# GOLD
## experience
**2ND EDITION**

EXAM PRACTICE

**C1**
Advanced

# EXAM OVERVIEW

The **Cambridge English Assessment: C1 Advanced**, is set at Level C1 on the CEFR (Common European Framework of Reference) scale. The exam is made up of **four papers**, each testing a different area of ability in English. If a candidate achieves an A grade, they will receive a Certificate in Advanced English stating that they demonstrated ability at Level C2. If a candidate achieves a grade B or C, they will receive the Certificate in Advanced English at Level C1. If a candidate only achieves a B2 level, they may receive a Cambridge English Certificate stating that they demonstrated ability at Level B2.

**Reading and Use of English:** 1 hour 30 minutes  **Listening:** 40 minutes (approximately)
**Writing:** 1 hour 30 minutes  **Speaking:** 15 minutes for each pair (approximately)

All the questions are task-based. Rubrics (instructions) are important and should be read carefully. They set the context and give important information about the tasks. There is a separate answer sheet for recording answers for the Reading and Use of English and Listening papers.

| Paper | Formats | Task focus |
|---|---|---|
| **Reading and Use of English** Eight parts 56 questions | **Part 1:** multiple-choice cloze. A text with eight gaps, and four options to choose from for each gap. | **Part 1:** use of vocabulary including idioms, fixed phrases, complementation, phrasal verbs. |
| | **Part 2:** open cloze. A text with eight gaps. Candidates write the correct word in each gap. | **Part 2:** use of grammar, vocabulary and expressions. |
| | **Part 3:** word formation. A text with eight gaps and a word at the end of the line in which the gap appears. Candidates write the correct form of this word in the gap. | **Part 3:** vocabulary, particularly prefixes and suffixes, changes in form and compound words. |
| | **Part 4:** key-word transformations. Candidates rewrite six sentences using a given word, so that they mean the same as the original sentences. | **Part 4:** use of grammatical and lexical structure. |
| | **Part 5:** multiple choice. A text with six four-option, multiple-choice questions. | **Part 5:** identify details, such as opinion, attitude, tone, purpose, main idea, text organisation and features. |
| | **Part 6:** cross-text multiple matching. Four short texts followed by four multiple-matching questions | **Part 6:** comparing and contrasting opinions and attitudes across four different texts. |
| | **Part 7:** gapped text. One long text with six paragraphs missing. Candidates replace paragraphs from a choice of seven. | **Part 7:** reading to understand cohesion, coherence, organisation and text structure. |
| | **Part 8:** multiple matching. A text or several short texts with ten multiple-matching questions. | **Part 8:** reading to locate specific information, detail, opinion and attitude. |
| **Writing** Two tasks, carrying equal marks. | **Part 1:** compulsory task. Using given information to write an essay of 220–260 words. | **Part 1:** writing an essay with a discursive focus based on two points given in the task. |
| | **Part 2:** Producing one piece of writing of 220–260 words, from a letter/email, proposal, review or report. | **Part 2:** writing for a specific target reader and context, using appropriate layout and register. |
| **Listening** Four tasks 30 questions | **Part 1:** multiple-choice questions. Three short dialogues with interacting speakers, with two multiple-choice questions (three options) per extract. | **Part 1:** understanding gist, detail, function, agreement, speaker purpose, feelings, attitude, etc. |
| | **Part 2:** sentence completion. One monologue with eight sentences to complete with a word or short phrase. | **Part 2:** locating and recording specific information and stated opinions. |
| | **Part 3:** multiple-choice questions. A conversation between two or more speakers, with six four-option multiple-choice questions. | **Part 3:** understanding attitude and opinion. |
| | **Part 4:** multiple matching. A set of five short monologues on a theme. There are two tasks. In both tasks candidates match each monologue to one of eight prompts. | **Part 4:** identifying main points, gist, attitude and opinion. |
| **Speaking** Four tasks | **Part 1:** examiner-led conversation. | **Part 1:** general social and interactional language |
| | **Part 2:** individual long turn with visual and written prompts. Candidates talk about two pictures from a choice of three. | **Part 2:** organising discourse, speculating, comparing, giving opinions. |
| | **Part 3:** two-way collaborative task. Candidates discuss a question with 5 written prompts and then answer a second question on the topic. | **Part 3:** sustaining interaction, expressing and justifying opinions, evaluating and speculating, negotiating towards a decision, etc. |
| | **Part 4:** The examiner asks questions related to the Part 3 topic. | **Part 4:** expressing and justifying ideas and opinions, agreeing and disagreeing, speculating. |

# CONTENTS

# PRACTICE TEST 1 WITH GUIDANCE

## About the paper

The *Reading and Use of English* paper lasts for 1 hour and 30 minutes. There are eight parts to the paper, and a total of 56 questions. You have to read texts of different types and different lengths, for example, extracts from newspapers, magazines, websites and novels, as well as other short texts.

### Part 1: Multiple-choice cloze

You read a short text and answer eight four-option multiple-choice questions. There are eight gaps in the text and you have to choose the word or phrase from a choice of four which fits best in each gap.

### Part 2: Open cloze

You read a short text and answer open-cloze questions. There are eight gaps in the text. You have to fill each gap with the missing word.

### Part 3: Word formation

You read a short text and answer eight word-formation questions. Eight words have been removed from the text. You're given the base form of each missing word at the end of the line. You have to make changes to the form of the word so that it makes sense in the gap.

### Part 4: Key word transformation

You read six pairs of sentences and answer key-word transformation questions. The pairs of sentences have the same meaning, but are expressed in different ways. There's a gap in the second sentence, which you have to fill with between three and six words. You're given one of these words, which is called the key word.

## How to do the paper

### Part 1

- Read the title and the text, ignoring the gaps, to get a general understanding.
- Read the options (A–D) for each question. Only one option fits the gap.
- Check the words before and after the gap. For example, some words can only be followed by one preposition, or may form part of a common collocation.
- Some questions focus on linking words, and you may need to understand the meaning of the whole text to know which word is correct in the context.
- If you're not sure which word to choose, go through and decide which options are clearly wrong. Then choose from the options that are left.
- When you've finished, read the whole text again and check that it makes sense with your answers in the gaps.

### Part 2

- Read the title and the text, ignoring the gaps, to get a general understanding.
- Think about the missing words. You only need to put one word in each gap. It's usually a grammatical word, for example, a pronoun, linker or preposition.
- Before you fill each gap, read the whole sentence carefully and think about the type of word that's missing, for example, it may be linking two ideas, or be part of a fixed phrase.
- When you've finished, read the whole text again and check that it makes complete sense with your answers in the gaps.

### Part 3

- Read the title and the text, ignoring the gaps, to get a general understanding.
- Think about the missing words. You only need to put one word in each gap, and the base form of that word is written in capital letters at the end of the line.
- Before you fill each gap, read the sentence carefully and think about the type of word that's missing. For example, is it a noun, an adjective, or an adverb?
- Change the word you've been given so that it fits the gap. You may need to add a prefix a suffix or make other changes.
- Check whether nouns need to be singular or plural, and that you've spelled the new word correctly.

### Part 4

- Read the first sentence carefully to make sure you understand exactly what it means.
- Look at the key word. What type of word is it? What usually follows it:: an infinitive, a preposition, or could it be part of a fixed phrase or phrasal verb?
- The second sentence often has the same information as the first sentence, expressed in a different order. Think about how the words need to change in the new order. For example, an adjective may become a noun or an adverb.
- You can include words and phrases in your answer that aren't used in the first sentence, but the meaning of the two sentences must be exactly the same.
- Remember that you cannot change the key word in any way.
- Check that your answer has between three and six words. Remember that contracted words count as two words. For example, *won't = will not*.
- Check that the two sentences have exactly the same meaning with your answer in the gap.

## About the paper

### Part 5: Multiple choice
There is one long text to read. You have to answer six multiple-choice questions, each with four options. The questions follow the order of information in the text.

### Part 6: Cross-text multiple matching
You read four short texts on the same topic. There are four questions which report the views and opinions of the different writers of the four texts. You have to match each question to the correct text or writer.

### Part 7: Gapped text
You read one long text from which six paragraphs have been removed. These paragraphs are placed in a jumbled order after the text, together with a seventh paragraph that doesn't fit in any of the gaps. You have to use your knowledge of grammar, vocabulary and referencing to work out which paragraph goes in each gap.

### Part 8: Multiple matching
There is either a long text divided into sections, or a series of short texts on the same topic. There are ten questions which report information and ideas from the text(s). You have to match each question to the correct section in the text.

## How to do the paper

### Part 5
- Read the title and text quickly to get a general understanding of what it's about and how it's organised.
- Read through the questions or question stems without looking at the options (A–D), and underline key words.
- The questions follow the order of the text. Find the section of text where the question is answered and read it carefully, underlining key words and phrases.
- Try to answer the question yourself. Then read the options A–D and choose the one that's closest to your own answer. Look for the same ideas expressed in different ways in the text and in the options.
- Check that the other options are definitely wrong. If you're still not completely sure, read the text again and go through and work out why the other options are wrong.

### Part 6
- Read the questions (37–40) first, underlining key words and ideas. There are two main types of question. In most questions you're told which section of text to read and which idea you're looking for. Do these questions first.
  - Read the section of text mentioned in the question and find the relevant topic or idea. Read this carefully to make sure you understand what the writer thinks about it.
  - The question then asks you to compare this writer's ideas or opinions on the topic with those of the other three writers. You may have to decide who has the same ideas and opinions, or who expresses different ones.
  - Now read the other texts carefully to find references to the topic or idea. Then read these sections carefully to make sure you've found the writer who has the same or different ideas or opinions.
- In the other type of question, you're told the topic or idea and asked to find the writer who has a different opinion to the others on that topic. Do this question last.
  - Read all the texts to find references to the topic or idea mentioned in the question.
  - Read the sections carefully to see which writer has different ideas to the other three on this topic.

### Part 7
- Read the title and text first, ignoring the gaps, to get a general idea of what it's about and how it's organised.
- Next, read the text around each gap carefully and think about the type of information which might be in the missing paragraph.
- Read paragraphs A–G. Check for topic and language links with the base text. Highlight words that relate to people, places and events, plus any time references. This will help you to follow the development of the argument or narrative.
- Choose the best option to fit each gap. Make sure that all the pronoun and vocabulary references are clear.
- Once you've finished, re-read the completed text to be sure that it makes sense with your answers in the gaps.

### Part 8
- You don't need to read the whole text or set of texts first.
- Read questions 47–56 first, underlining key words and ideas.
- Read through the text(s) quickly and find information or ideas that are relevant to each question.
- For each question, when you find the relevant piece of text, read it very carefully to make sure that it completely matches the meaning of the question.
- You'll probably find references to the ideas in the questions in more than one section of the text, but only one section exactly matches the idea in the question. You need to read all these sections carefully to find the exact match.

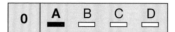

## Part I

For questions **1 – 8**, read the text below and decide which answer (**A, B, C** or **D**) best fits each gap. There is an example at the beginning (**0**).

In the exam, you mark your answers **on a separate answer sheet**.

**Example:**

| 0 | **A** whole | **B** total | **C** mass | **D** sum |

| 0 | A — | B ☐ | C ☐ | D ☐ |

**TIP STRIP**

**Question 1:** Which of these adjectives can be followed by the preposition *of*?

**Question 2:** Which of these words commonly collocates with *related to*?

**Question 5:** Look at the sentence after the gap and think about the meaning. Which expression will provide the contrast here?

**Question 7:** Only one of these words can be followed by the infinitive form of the verb.

# Sleep is good for you

If you look at the population as a **(0)** .......... , it is evident that people need differing amounts of sleep. Generally speaking, however, the younger you are, the more sleep you're likely to need, and this is **(1)** .......... of both humans and many animal species. Young children also tend to sleep more deeply than adults and this may be **(2)** .......... related to the fact that their brains are still developing. During deep sleep, the brain is busy processing new information and getting ready to **(3)** .......... newly learnt skills into practice in waking life.

It has also been established that changes **(4)** .......... in sleep patterns during adolescence. Gradually, the sleep of teenagers becomes shallower, **(5)** .......... teenagers still need more sleep than their parents. Researchers have **(6)** .......... to the fact that as people age, there's a **(7)** .......... to find the acquisition of new skills more challenging, and this is seen as **(8)** .......... evidence of the relationship between sleep and mental agility that is observed in teenagers.

| 1 | **A** correct | **B** true | **C** right | **D** valid |
|---|---|---|---|---|
| 2 | **A** surely | **B** tightly | **C** closely | **D** greatly |
| 3 | **A** send | **B** take | **C** bring | **D** put |
| 4 | **A** occur | **B** exhibit | **C** manifest | **D** enter |
| 5 | **A** as well as | **B** even though | **C** apart from | **D** regardless |
| 6 | **A** revealed | **B** suggested | **C** acknowledged | **D** pointed |
| 7 | **A** tendency | **B** likelihood | **C** trend | **D** liability |
| 8 | **A** greater | **B** deeper | **C** wider | **D** further |

## Part 2

For questions **9 – 16**, read the text below and think of the word which best fits each gap. Use only one word in each gap. There is an example at the beginning (**0**).

In the exam, you write your answers **IN CAPITAL LETTERS on a separate answer sheet**.

**Example:** | 0 | T | O | | | | | | | | | | | | | | | | | |

---

# Running for beginners

According **(0)** .......... press reports, running is fast becoming one of the most popular participant sports. But how easy is it for beginners to **(9)** .......... up running, and are there any pitfalls to be avoided at **(10)** .......... costs?

Apparently, **(11)** .......... many novices go wrong is in setting themselves unrealistic goals. Professional coaches advise an initial running regime in **(12)** .......... just a minute's running is followed by a minute's walking, so that stamina can be built up gradually. Over time, the spurts of running can gradually be lengthened **(13)** .......... the expense of the walking breaks, until a realistic target is reached.

Another common mistake is trying to run too fast. **(14)** .......... can really help in this respect is a more experienced running partner, who can help to set and moderate the pace. **(15)** .......... a rule of thumb, if you're **(16)** .......... to talk comfortably to a partner without feeling out of breath, then your running speed isn't appropriate for your level of fitness, and you need to slow down.

**TIP STRIP**

**Question 9:** A verb is needed here to make a phrasal verb with the preposition *up*.

**Question 11:** A relative pronoun is needed here.

**Question 13:** Which preposition completes this common expression?

**Question 16:** Read the sentence carefully. Is a positive or negative form needed here?

## Part 3

For questions **17 – 24**, read the text below. Use the word given in capitals at the end of some of the lines to form a word that fits in the gap in the same line. There is an example at the beginning (**0**).

In the exam, you write your answers **IN CAPITAL LETTERS on a separate answer sheet**.

**Example:**

| 0 | E | X | T | R | E | M | E | L | Y | | | | | | | | | |

---

# The celebrity biography

The celebrity biography is an **(0)** ........... popular literary genre. It provides a ready source of income for many writers who might otherwise find themselves unemployed in a very **(17)** ........... industry.

**EXTREME**

**COMPETE**

The problem with writing the biography of a living person, however, is that you're very **(18)** ........... on the celebrity for information. Unless that person sees the book as an opportunity to reveal previously **(19)** ........... secrets about their private life, the actual material can be **(20)** ........... dull, with the result that the book itself becomes a simple **(21)** ........... together of known facts.

**RELY**

**SUSPECT**

**DISAPPOINT**

**GATHER**

Much more exciting from the writer's point of view is embarking on the biography of a celebrity from the past. You're often given access to the celebrity's private **(22)** ..........., which may contain letters that have been lying unread for years. Although going through them is quite a **(23)** ........... process, there is always the chance of gaining a real **(24)** ........... into the person's true character or, even better, a hint of scandal.

**CORRESPOND**

**LABOUR**

**SIGHT**

For questions **25 – 30**, complete the second sentence so that it has a similar meaning to the first sentence, using the word given. **Do not change the word given.** You must use between three and six words, including the word given. Here is an example (**0**).

**Example:**

**0**   **Amy** stayed at the hotel once before.

   **FIRST**

   This ............................................................... Amy has stayed at the hotel.

The gap can be filled with the words 'is not the first time that', so you write:

| Example: | 0 | IS NOT THE FIRST TIME THAT |
|---|---|---|

In the exam, you write **only** the missing words **IN CAPITAL LETTERS on a separate answer sheet.**

---

**25**   Dan applied for the job even though he didn't have the necessary qualifications.

   **SPITE**

   Dan applied for the job ................................................ he lacked the necessary qualifications.

**26**   I really don't mind whether I play in the match or not.

   **DIFFERENCE**

   It really ............................................... me whether I play in the match or not.

**27**   **Without** my parent's support, I'd never have managed to win the gold medal.

   **BEEN**

   If it ............................................... of my parents, I'd never have managed to win the gold medal.

**28**   Sam wasn't the only student on the course who found the assignment challenging.

   **ALONE**

   Amongst students on the course, Sam ............................................... the assignment challenging.

**29**   Would you mind if other people used your desk while you're away on holiday?

   **OBJECTION**

   Would ............................................... other people using your desk while you're away on holiday?

**30**   You should consider all the options before coming to a conclusion.

   **TAKEN**

   All the options ............................................... before you come to a conclusion.

**TIP STRIP**

**Question 25:** You need a phrase that means the same as 'despite'.

**Question 27:** You need to use the past perfect tense in your answer.

**Question 29:** *alone* is followed by a preposition and a gerund.

**Question 30:** You need to change *consider* into a noun.

**Part 5**

You are going to read an article about an exhibition. For questions **31 – 36**, choose the answer (**A, B, C** or **D**) which you think fits best according to the text.

In the exam, you mark your answers **on a separate answer sheet**.

---

## The Spark of Life

*A new exhibition revisits the pioneering days of mass electricity.*

The *Spark of Life* exhibition sets out to show how an understanding of electricity lies at the heart of modern existence. But as well as showing how mankind has struggled to understand and harness this invisible but powerful force of nature, it also invites us to consider some of the everyday manifestations that mark the success of that struggle. In charting the social history of electricity, and by focusing on the history of such prosaic items as light bulbs and electricity pylons, it skillfully brings home to us the extent to which such things have transformed the world we live in.

For example, we hear that when the architects of Manchester's impressive John Rylands Library were planning its interior illumination in the 1890s, suppliers of electric lamps were battling to supplant gas lighting in homes and workplaces, claiming that it provided a softer and steadier glow. They triumphed at the Rylands by successfully arguing that electricity would be less likely to have a detrimental effect on its precious volumes than fume-generating gas lights. When the library opened in 1900 with its own generator, it was one of Britain's first public buildings to be lit entirely by electricity.

The splendid floral designs for the Rylands light fittings, made of gunmetal and bronze, are on show in the *Spark of Life* exhibition. They were designed to harmonise with the tulip-shaped bulbs prevalent at the time. Amazingly, a few of the Rylands' original incandescent bulbs survived in place until 1995, when the library was finally upgraded to a modern electricity supply. They, too, will be in the exhibition, lent by Manchester's Museum of Science and Industry. The earliest bulbs have long-lasting carbon filaments, like those patented by Thomas Edison in 1880, and feature the little glass pips that sealed early bulbs. They have no factory marks, but it is likely that they were hand-blown to order, says curator Alice Cliff. Their illumination would have been similar to a modern 15-watt incandescent bulb. Whether they would light up today when connected to a power supply remains unknown, as the museum is unwilling to risk such an experiment. In those pioneering days of electricity, light bulbs had a certain decorative glamour, which disappeared as they became cheap commodity items. Today, however, their appeal is returning as new materials technology makes it possible to create long-life, low-energy filaments in wonderful patterns.

The exhibition also looks at how electricity was distributed from power stations through cables, first within cities and then across nations, so that on-site generators like that at the Rylands Library were no longer needed. The star exhibit is a collection of photographs of pylons around the world taken in the 1920s, the heyday of mass electrification. It turned up in the Science Museum archives at Wroughton, says Ruth Garde, the show's curator, but sadly without any clue as to the identity of the photographers or why it was originally put together. The photographs illustrate the popular excitement associated with those early pylons as they
line 26 swooped across landscapes, bringing power to the masses.

The *Los Angeles Times* described an early Californian transmission line in 1913: "Electric energy from the far-off Sierras stretched
line 28 a hand robed with lightning across the gulf of valleys and mountains to the doors of the city." A decade later, the Chicago architect EH Bennett said: "To the mind of any imagination there is at times something irresistible in the aspect of great airy structures
line 30 stalking the hills." While Britain's 'pylon poets' such as Stephen Spender celebrated them as symbols of technological progress,
line 31 other campaigners lamented the scarring of the landscape. But any such misgivings failed to halt construction and, by the 1940s, the UK had one of Europe's most extensive and reliable electricity networks.

The UK had come came relatively late to the pylon party. In 1926, it was lagging well behind France and Germany in mass electrification, when the government set up a national body known as the National Grid to oversee the process. In 1928, a committee headed by anti-modernist architect Sir Reginald Blomfield came up with the open-lattice tower design, based on an American model. This has been the standard pylon for the UK grid and a familiar feature of the landscape ever since. Today, pylons are low on the list of most people's interests, though the UK does have a Pylon Appreciation Society. But new overhead lines will be needed in future, and the National Grid is hedging its bets. For some lines it will stick with the traditional steel lattice pylons, whilst for others it plans to introduce the new Danish T-pylon – a solid pole with cross arms from which the power lines are suspended in diamond-shaped structures. Is a new debate about the design of power delivery about to be sparked?

**31**    In the first paragraph, the writer praises the exhibition for

    **A**    focusing on such unusual examples of technical creativity.

    **B**    making a rather challenging topic accessible to non-specialists.

    **C**    relating the development of familiar objects to much wider themes.

    **D**    highlighting how difficult it is to imagine a world without electricity.

**32**    In the second paragraph, we learn that the architects of the John Rylands Library decided to adopt electric lighting because

    **A**    it was less likely to damage the building's contents.

    **B**    it provided better illumination for the building's users.

    **C**    it had been successfully used in other types of buildings.

    **D**    it could draw on another of the building's innovative features.

**33**    What is suggested about the oldest light bulbs at the exhibition?

    **A**    They may still prove to be in good working order.

    **B**    It might be possible to find out exactly who made them.

    **C**    They were individually designed to match particular light fittings.

    **D**    It is regrettable that they were removed from their original setting.

**34**    What is known about the collection of photographs in the exhibition?

    **A**    It was gathered together to present a positive image of electricity.

    **B**    It features the work of people who chose to remain anonymous.

    **C**    It sets out to show why pylons became so common worldwide.

    **D**    It dates from a boom period in the history of electricity.

**35**    Which of the following phrases is used to suggest disapproval?

    **A**    swooped across (line 26)

    **B**    robed with lightning (line 28)

    **C**    stalking the hills (line 30)

    **D**    scarring of the landscape (line 31)

**36**    In the last paragraph, the writer suggests that in future, pylons in the UK

    **A**    will be replaced by much less obtrusive structures.

    **B**    may become more varied in their appearance.

    **C**    are unlikely to attract much public attention.

    **D**    may be less attractive than those of the past.

**TIP STRIP**

**Question 31:** Look for a word in the paragraph that expresses how well the exhibition fulfils its aims.

**Question 32:** Be careful. You are looking for the reason behind the decision.

**Question 35:** Read what comes after each of the phrases in the article to find the answer.

You are going to read four extracts from reviews of a book about a house in London. For questions **37 – 40**, choose from the reviewers **A – D**. The reviewers may be chosen more than once.

In the exam, you mark your answers on **a separate answer sheet**.

---

### *The House by the Thames* by Gillian Tindall

#### Reviewer A

London has witnessed successive waves of demolition and rebuilding as rich citizens responded to changes in architectural fashion. It's remarkable, therefore, that one old house on the south bank of the River Thames opposite St. Paul's Cathedral should have survived. What happened in and around this house forms the spindle around which Ms. Tindall spins a series of delicately crafted tales. Thanks to her painstaking research, we are presented with an enormously detailed account of the lives of the people who have lived in the house since the 16th century. Had it been a simple chronological account, we might have got bogged down in all this detail, but the deft interweaving of the stories themselves keeps you turning the page. For me, however, the work is essentially episodic. I was expecting it all to be leading somewhere, for some conclusion to be drawn from all this detail, but it never came.

#### Reviewer B

Gillian Tindall has produced a history of London viewed through the microcosm of one house and the people who lived in it. I found myself enthralled from page one, carried along as much by the elegance of the prose as by the narrative itself. Tindall's achievement is all the more remarkable because the stories she tells are true ones and the house still exists. It's a triumph of thorough research, which makes you want to unearth the story of your own house, although there were times when the sheer volume of factual information was a little indigestible, and I did skip the odd page. The way that Tindall returns to various central themes in the history of London as the story of the house unfolds is, however, very effective. It forces you to reconsider not only your understanding of history, but what history itself is.

#### Reviewer C

I was recommended this book by a friend. I didn't really know what to expect, but I'm certainly grateful for the recommendation. The history of the house is learnedly told, from its origins as a 16th-century inn through to its unlikely 20th-century survival despite the ravages of war and economic upheaval. Tindall's style of writing is a little bit old-fashioned for my taste, however, and I found it off-putting in places. Another problem I had was that the structure of the book itself is quite complicated, so I had to keep looking backwards and forwards to remember who was who and where they fitted into the story. But having said that, I came away having learnt a wealth of new and fascinating information about everyday life in London across the centuries. What's more, in charting the history of one London house and its inhabitants, Gillian Tindall's thought-provoking book shows us just how much history is the sum of its parts.

#### Reviewer D

Tindall is the sort of writer you wish you could meet and get to know personally. There's something about the clear way she expresses her ideas that I find very accessible and reassuring. In order to write this book, she must have spent a lot of time in libraries and dusty archives. It's staggering to think that so much information still exists about people who lived long ago, if you know where to look. I'm full of admiration for her patience, but sometimes I felt a bit overloaded – as if she wanted to tell me every little fact she'd found. The way the story is told is quite clever, sometimes focusing on the house and sometimes on the people, but I'm afraid I did lose the thread at times. For me, the strength of the book lies in the fact that it made me realise that big events and trends really do affect the lives of ordinary people, and that's something we shouldn't underestimate or shy away from.

**Which reviewer**

has a different view from Reviewer D regarding the effect the writer's use of language has on the reader? **37** ☐

expresses a similar view to Reviewer B about whether the level of detail in the book is appropriate? **38** ☐

has a similar view to Reviewer C about how easy it is to follow the stories in the book? **39** ☐

expresses a different view to the others about the extent to which the book raises issues of wider significance? **40** ☐

**TIP STRIP**

**Question 37:** Reviewer D says that the writer expresses her ideas in a clear way. Look at what the other reviewers say about the way the book is written. Which one didn't like the style of writing?

**Question 38:** Reviewer B says "the sheer volume of factual information was a little indigestible." Look at the other reviewers to see who also found the book too detailed.

**Question 40:** Each reviewer ends by commenting on the wider issues raised by the book. Which one feels these were not sufficiently dealt with?

## Part 7

You are going to read an article about a winter sports holiday. Six paragraphs have been removed from the article. Choose from the paragraphs **A – G** the one which fits each gap (**41 – 46**). There is one extra paragraph which you do not need to use.

In the exam, you mark your answers **on a separate answer sheet**.

---

## Ski safari

*Our reporter samples a different type of winter sports holiday.*

It was only when the doors of the carriage slid open that we fully realised what sort of a day lay in store for us. Passengers on this route normally pop out like corks from a bottle when it reaches its destination, eager to snap on their skis and be first on the descent. Today, though, our fellow travellers paused momentarily on the threshold as a vicious gale whipped icy particles into their faces at -25⁰C, one or two shivering before setting their shoulders against the blast.

**41**

That left us with no choice but to take the rack railway that's been winding its way up to 3,089 metres in all weathers since 1898. Flexibility, and a willingness to use any transport available, would be the keys to our trip. We were embarking on a 'ski safari' — an increasingly popular style of Alpine adventure designed to revive the spirits of the mountain enthusiast who's grown weary of winter sports resorts.

**42**

The customisable character of this arrangement means that groups can choose exactly how vigorously — or languidly — they want to proceed, settle on their consensus fitness level and decide whether the priority is clocking up the ski miles, communing with nature or sampling the local cuisine over long lunches.

**43**

Expansion into winter tourism is a recent venture, seizing on the ski safari concept as a way of standing out from the competition — despite the inevitable logistical headaches that come with combining complicated itineraries with fickle high-altitude weather.

Our plan was to spend the morning exploring the off-piste options around the railhead, before making our way up to a mountain refuge for the night. The sight of so much snow swirling around had also raised hopes of skiing on fresh powder. But our guides had to find it first.

**44**

Fortunately, conditions were on the turn: with every few metres we descended, the breeze dropped slightly and visibility improved. Our guides suddenly dropped off the edge of the piste into a vale of untouched snow.

**45**

After a day of mini-adventures — including being occasionally thrown off-balance by the weight of rucksacks carrying avalanche airbags, shovels, probes and transceivers, as well as our night-time gear — our windswept crew drew up to the mountain refuge. Built in 1885, this was a relic of the pioneering days of winter sports.

**46**

For some, the chief flaw of such places is the shock of the unheated dorm. True, the air was bitingly cold as I climbed into my bunk. Within minutes, however, I was asleep, snug under a heavy-duty duvet. We awoke the next day to find the storm had broken. The descent was euphoric, our fat skis carving easily through the shin-deep powder on the upper slopes, which lower down gave way to denser, wetter snow — a choppier business altogether — but the experience of peak-to-valley fresh tracks was hard to beat.

Would I do it again? Without hesitation. It's hard to imagine a better antidote to the routine week's ski package.

**A** There were surprises lurking here and there under the surface as we set off in hot pursuit, but the occasional jolt underfoot seemed like a price worth paying for finally being let off the leash. As the lift system gradually reopened, we worked our way towards our destination for the night.

**B** The former took precedence amongst most of our group, which consisted of several expert skiers, including our hosts from the travel company, which has long experience of running summer holidays at its beach club in Greece.

**C** Yet it requires a relaxed approach. If you worry too much about the logistics and objectives, you're getting it all wrong. But go with the flow, and you never know where it might take you.

**D** Looking upwards, one of them pointed to a mountainside that two days earlier had been knee-deep in the stuff. Since then, the raging storm had simply picked it up and deposited it elsewhere, leaving the slope looking as if it was still early in the season, with treetops and rocks poking out of a sandblasted base.

**E** It rests on a simple but enticing concept: rather than stay in one place, you make a journey on skis, using cable cars, helicopters, skidoos and anything else available to 'daisy-chain' across valleys and ridges, staying in different villages or mountain huts as you go.

**F** Despite lying within sight of pisted slopes and the cable car, it upholds all the best traditions of the genre. At night, the fug of the dining room was almost overwhelming, a wood-fired stove pumping heat to radiators liberally draped with our kit.

**G** An hour earlier, we'd been sipping coffee and lounging on sofas in the well-appointed boot room of the hotel down in Zermatt. On the wall, a video screen showed that high winds had closed all the main chairlifts and cable cars.

**TIP STRIP**

**Question 41:** Read the sentence in the paragraph after the gap. Now find the option that talks about why the writer took the train.

**Question 42:** The text before the gap introduces the idea of a ski safari. Look for the paragraph that explains how it is organised.

**Question 43:** The text before the gap talks about different options. Look for the paragraph which uses a word that picks up on this idea.

**Question 45:** Look for the paragraph that contains a phrase that refers to the words *our guides* before the gap.

## Part 8

You are going to read an article about astronomy. For questions **47 – 56**, choose from the sections of the article (**A – D**). The sections may be chosen more than once.

In the exam, you mark your answers **on a separate answer sheet**.

---

**In which section does the writer mention**

| | |
|---|---|
| a piece of equipment that's surprisingly easy to move? | **47** |
| the motivation behind this particular trip to visit his relative? | **48** |
| how preparing for an outdoor astronomy session can improve results? | **49** |
| how astronomers can become completely absorbed in the activity? | **50** |
| a philosophical attitude towards a frustrating aspect of astronomy? | **51** |
| how the level of cloud cover isn't the only factor that can affect visibility? | **52** |
| the range of things a beginner might now expect to observe with ease? | **53** |
| how methods of getting to know the night sky have changed? | **54** |
| an expression that astronomers use for a very satisfying experience? | **55** |
| something that reveals that he isn't a complete novice as an astronomer? | **56** |

### TIP STRIP

**Question 47:** Look at the texts and underline places where pieces of equipment are mentioned. Where is this particular point made?

**Question 49:** All the sections talk about being outdoors, but which of them mentions something that was done to improve the results of the session?

**Question 51:** Look for sections of text that describe situations that astronomers might find frustrating. Read these sections carefully to find the attitude described in the question.

**Question 56:** The word *novice* means 'beginner'. The word occurs in section B, but this isn't the answer. Find the text where the writer tells us something that shows he has done some astronomy before.

# My stargazing trip

I spent the night with my uncle Jon, who's a keen astronomer.

**A**

It's approaching ten o'clock on a winter's night and I'm outdoors, on a pebble beach on the English coast. Most sensible people are safely indoors, but I'm trying to shelter from the rain behind a giant telescope. I've arranged to meet my uncle Jon, a keen astronomer, here. His house is within a stone's throw of the sea and so our plan is to spend the evening on the beach in a celestial huddle. My own modest telescope has been gathering dust for years, but I'm hoping Jon might inspire me to gaze at the heavens more often. The astronomer's good luck motto is 'clear skies'. However, tonight the stars are hidden behind a thin layer of cloud. Jon's not easily disheartened, however. "That's all part of astronomy. It makes those beautiful clear evenings even more memorable. You have to be patient and accept that clouds are a natural, if rather annoying, phenomenon for us. This is still a very unfriendly sky."

**B**

While we sip tea on the beach and search for the first twinkle of a star, Jon explains that most telescopes are now fitted with a computer 'brain' that uses satellite technology to grab a fix on their location. The unit can factor in the time and date to give a telescope a built-in chart of the sky. Astronomers then key in which object they want to view, and a series of tiny motors rotate the telescope so it points to the exact location in the galaxy. "I didn't have all that when I was a kid, so I found my way around the universe using books and maps," says Jon. "I can still remember how amazed I was when I saw the surface of the Moon for the first time. Nowadays, a novice can pick up a relatively reasonably priced telescope and be marvelling at Saturn or Venus within a few minutes and then move onto the major constellations."

**C**

As the clouds start to thin, Jon shows me the huge telescope that he's selected from his impressive collection. Despite being more than a metre long and attached to a solid tripod, it's remarkably mobile. The unit has been left outside for most of the evening to adapt to the temperature. This helps remove heat from the inner components, allowing the air in the optical path to stabilise and give a clearer image of the stars. For now, though, all we can see through our lens is an overcast sky. "Astronomers have a little language of their own," explains Jon. Clear skies are one thing, but 'the seeing' has to be good as well. This depends on how turbulent the atmosphere is and can be spoilt by a rippling or 'jellyfish' effect through the lens.

**D**

Jon says that if you want to try your hand at stargazing before investing large sums on a telescope, a pair of traditional binoculars is good for viewing the Moon. "Even now I still marvel at how vivid the edge of the craters are. But I'd also say buy some warm clothes because astronomy can get compulsive. I've been up looking at the stars until 5a.m., totally oblivious." Just as it seems we aren't going to see further than a few thousand metres, a tiny window of moonlight is reflected on the surface of the sea. Slowly, almost magically, it starts to move towards us on the shore, as the clouds separate and drift with the breeze. Jon swings the telescope around and we have a clear view of the Moon. Everyone's seen footage of the Apollo missions, and there are plenty of NASA pictures out there, but to view it through a telescope is still breathtaking. But then the clouds move in again swiftly, the rain sheets down and we're left in darkness. Jon's as excited as me. "When you see an object through a particular telescope for the first time, that's called 'first light'. It's a very special moment and you can be moved to tears. When you realise what's out there in the galaxy, it puts things in perspective and it can be a humbling experience too."

# GUIDANCE: WRITING

## About the paper

The *Writing* paper lasts for 1 hour 30 minutes. There are two parts to the paper, and in each part you complete one task. All the tasks carry equal marks.

### Part 1

**This is compulsory and you have to write an essay**. There's one task with three points and some notes. You choose two of these three points and discuss them in your essay, using information from the input text or notes. You have to explain which of your chosen two points you agree with or feel is most important, and give reasons for your opinion. You should write between 220 and 260 words.

### Part 2

**This has three questions and you choose one question to answer**. The choice may include a letter or an email, a proposal, a report or a review. You are given a clear context, an indication of what to include and a reason for writing in each question. You should write between 220 and 260 words.

## How to do the paper

### General points

- Spend around five minutes planning your writing. You won't have enough time to write a rough answer and then a final, clean copy in the exam, but if you plan well, this won't be necessary.
- Make sure your writing is legible, and that your answer is the correct length. If you write too much, you might include irrelevant information, which could confuse the reader and have a negative effect. If your answer is too short, you may not cover all the points in the question.
- Make sure your answer has a clear beginning and end so that it is well-organised and is easy to follow.
- Use a range of language, including a variety of vocabulary and some complex grammatical structures, in an appropriate register and style for the task.
- Check your finished answer. Make sure you've included the necessary information, given enough detail for each point and you haven't made careless mistakes.

### Part 1

- Read the instructions carefully so that you know what to write.
- Check that you understand the situation, the context and all the points you have been given in the task.
- Plan your answer. Make sure that you have enough to say about the points you choose and that you can think of reasons or examples to support your argument. You can use the opinions given in the task, or you can use your own if you prefer.
- Don't copy words or phrases from the input texts, and remember to write in a formal style.

### Part 2

- Read all the questions before you decide which one to answer. Think about what each question means and the style of writing required.
- Each task has a specified target reader and reason for writing. This tells you the register and kind of language to use.
- Think about the type of writing you are best at. If you like formal language and expressing ideas, consider writing a report or a proposal.
- If you like trying to interest your reader you may choose a review.
- Think about each task carefully before you write. Have you enough ideas for the topic? Would you enjoy writing in the style required?

## Testing focus

Both parts of the *Writing* paper carry equal marks.
Spelling, punctuation, length, paragraphing, and legible handwriting are taken into account in both parts of the test.

The examiner will consider the following:

- **Content**: How well have you fulfilled the task? Have you included relevant information and answered the question?
- **Communicative achievement**: How appropriate is the writing for the type of task? Is the register appropriate?
- **Organisation**: Are your ideas organised logically and linked with appropriate connectors, and is the answer easy to follow?
- **Language**: Have you accurately used a range of vocabulary and grammatical structures, including some complex ones and a range of tenses?

# Part I

You **must** answer this question. Write your answer in **220 – 260** words in an appropriate style.

In the exam, you write your answer **on a separate answer sheet**.

1    Your class has held a debate on whether travelling to other countries is really necessary these days. You have made the notes below:

> ### Why do people travel to other countries these days?
>
> - on holiday
> - for business
> - cultural understanding
>
> > Some opinions expressed in the debate:
> >
> > "It's more exciting to go on holiday in another country than to stay at home."
> >
> > "It's vital to make business contacts, but this can also be done on the internet."
> >
> > "We live in a global world and it's important that we understand other cultures."

Write an essay discussing **two** of the points in your notes. You should **explain which one you think is most important, giving reasons** to support your opinion.

You may, if you wish, make use of the opinions expressed in the debate, but you should use your own words as far as possible.

## TIP STRIP

- Read the task carefully, and make sure you understand the topic of the essay.
- Read the notes and decide which two points you have most ideas about. Make your own notes on what you could write about. For example, *holidays in other countries are more relaxing; face-to-face meetings and web conferences via the internet are very effective; if we don't understand other cultures then we can't do business very well.*
- Plan your whole answer, including the conclusion. This is important because your essay should move towards the conclusion clearly and logically.
- Write your introduction so that you engage the reader immediately. You could do this by rephrasing the task as a rhetorical question. For example, *does this mean that it's necessary to travel to other countries or not?*
- Use a variety of grammatical structures in your essay, and remember to use a formal style.
- When you've finished, check that you've dealt with two of the points in enough detail and that your conclusion is clear.
- Finally, check your essay for any grammar or spelling mistakes.

## Part 2

Write an answer to **one** of the questions **2 – 4** in this part. Write your answer in **220 – 260** words in an appropriate style.

In the exam, you write your answer **on a separate answer sheet**. Put the question number in the box at the top of the answer sheet.

---

**2** The town council where you live would like to hold a weekend festival that would bring international visitors to the area. Local residents have been asked for proposals for the kinds of events that could be included in the festival, and suggestions for any extra facilities that would be required to make the town more attractive to tourists.

Write your **proposal**.

**3** You see the following announcement on the website of a new television channel.

# Reviews wanted

We want viewers to know what you think about our new nature channel! Send us reviews of a nature programme you have seen, saying whether you learned anything new from the programme and why you did or didn't enjoy it. Would you recommend the channel to others?

We'll post the most interesting reviews on our website.

Write your **review**.

**4** You have received an email from an English friend.

> ✉ 🔍
>
> Hello,
>
> Guess what – I've been selected for the hockey team and we're playing your college next weekend! Will you be playing or watching?
>
> It'd be great to meet up. I'd like to talk to you about what I'm thinking about doing in the future, which is to become a hockey coach. Any thoughts on whether it's a good career? Could you find out anything for me?
>
> See you soon,
>
> Jane

Write your **email** in reply.

### TIP STRIP

Read all the questions to decide which one you can answer best.

**Question 2:** Give recommendations and reasons, e.g. *they would create a community spirit.* State the purpose in the introduction. Include a variety of structures and complex language, even if you use bullet points. Finish by stating why your proposal should be adopted.

**Question 3:** Use semi-formal language. Decide which aspects made such a lasting impression, e.g. *it made me think about my own life.* Remember that people want to know whether to read the book, so end with your final opinion.

**Question 4:** Use an informal style with full sentences. Cover all the points from Jane's email and add your own details. Give advice and reassure her, e.g. *I have no doubt that ...* Begin and end your email appropriately.

# GUIDANCE: LISTENING

## About the paper

The *Listening* paper lasts for about 40 minutes. There are four parts and a total of 30 questions.

You listen to texts of different types and different lengths, for example extracts from media broadcasts and podcasts, as well as everyday conversations. You hear each recording twice and you have time to read the questions before you listen.

### Part 1: Multiple choice

You listen to three unrelated extracts of around one minute each. Each extract has two speakers. You have to answer two three-option, multiple-choice questions on each extract. The three extracts aren't linked in any way, and there's a variety of contexts and interaction patterns.

### Part 2: Sentence completion

You listen to one long monologue of around two to three minutes. The speaker is talking about a particular subject. A set of eight sentences report the speaker's main points. A word or short phrase has been removed from each sentence. You have to listen and complete the gaps.

### Part 3: Multiple choice

You listen to one long interview or discussion of around four minutes and answer six four-option, multiple-choice questions.

### Part 4: Multiple matching

You hear a series of five short monologues on a theme. Each monologue lasts around 30 seconds. You have to complete two tasks as you listen. Each task has eight options (A–H). As you listen, you match one option from Task 1 and one option from Task 2 to each speaker. You match the ideas that the speakers express to the wording of the options.

## How to do the paper

### Part 1

*   Before you listen to each extract, you hear the context sentence. Think about who the speakers are, what the topic is and the type of interaction you're going to hear. For example, is it an interview, an informal conversation, etc.?
*   You have time to read the two questions. Underline the main words and ideas in each question stem and options (A–C).
*   The question often tells you which of the speakers (the man, the woman or both) you need to listen to when you answer each question.
*   The first time you listen, find the correct answer to the question posed in the question stem.
*   The second time you listen, choose the option which matches your answer.
*   The wording of the options doesn't repeat the vocabulary and expressions used by the speakers. You need to match the meaning of ideas expressed in the recording to the wording of the questions.

### Part 2

*   Before you listen, you hear the context sentence. Think about the person who's speaking and the topic you're going to hear about.
*   You have 45 seconds to read through the sentences before you listen. Think about the type of information that is missing in each sentence.
*   Most answers are concrete pieces of information, for example, proper nouns.
*   The sentences you read are in the same order as the information you hear. Use these sentences to help you keep your place as you listen.
*   You hear the words you need to write on the recording. There's no need to change the form of the word or to find a paraphrase.
*   You should write no more than three words in each gap. Most answers are single words or compound nouns.
*   Check that your answer fits the sentence grammatically and makes sense in the complete sentence.

### Part 3

*   Before you listen, you hear the context sentence. Think about the people who are speaking and the topic you're going to hear about.
*   You have 70 seconds to read through all the questions before you listen.
*   Underline the main words and ideas in each question stem and options (A–D).
*   The questions follow the order of information in the recording. Listen out for key vocabulary and ideas that introduce the topic of each question. These are often in the interviewer's questions.
*   The questions often tell you which of the speakers (the man, the woman or both) you need to listen to when you answer each of the questions.
*   The first time you listen, find the correct answer to the question posed in the question stem.
*   The second time you listen, choose the option which matches your answer.
*   The wording of the options doesn't repeat the vocabulary and expressions used by the speakers. You need to match the meaning of ideas expressed in the recording to the wording of the questions.

### Part 4

*   There are five monologues on a theme. In each monologue, you hear a different speaker. You hear all five speakers once, then the series is repeated.
*   Before you listen, you hear the context sentence and the instructions for each of the two tasks. Think about the topic you're going to hear about, and the ideas you have to listen for.
*   You have 45 seconds to read through the two tasks before you listen. Read the options (A–H) in both tasks so that you're ready to choose one from each set for each speaker as you listen.
*   The first time you listen, pay attention to the speaker's main idea. Mark the option closest to this idea.
*   The second time you listen, check your answers. You may need to change some of them. Remember that in each task there are three options that you don't need to use.
*   Don't worry if you don't understand every word. If you're not sure of an answer, then guess. You've probably understood more than you think.

## Part 1

You will hear three different extracts. For questions **1 – 6**, choose the answer (**A, B** or **C**) which fits best according to what you hear. There are two questions for each extract.

In the exam, you write your answers on **a separate answer sheet**.

### Extract One

You hear two friends discussing the issue of noise pollution.

**1**   The woman questions the man's assumption that

    **A**   all kinds of noise are equally disturbing.

    **B**   living with continuous noise is unhealthy.

    **C**   noise pollution is as harmful as air pollution.

**2**   She's read that sleep is most often affected by noises which

    **A**   slowly get louder or softer.

    **B**   are intended to wake us up.

    **C**   don't follow a regular pattern.

### Extract Two

You hear part of a discussion about going to the cinema.

**3**   What makes the woman feel most uncomfortable in the cinema?

    **A**   The volume of the sound in some sequences.

    **B**   The kind of images featured in the advertising.

    **C**   The insensitivity of some members of the audience.

**4**   The man suggests that the selling of snacks in cinemas

    **A**   may be affecting audience numbers negatively.

    **B**   might be promoted by some forms of advertising.

    **C**   could be having an unexpected effect on customers.

### TIP STRIP

**Question 1:** The word *questions* means 'suggests it may not be correct'.

**Question 2:** Listen for what she says about 'sleep rhythms'.

**Question 4:** She uses the phrase *get on my nerves.* What is she referring to?

**Question 6:** You're listening for something that both speakers thought was true in the presentation.

**Extract Three**

You hear two friends discussing a presentation about language learning which they watched online.

5    Initially, the woman thought that the presenter was going to

**A**    spend too much time describing his own experiences.

**B**    be too lacking in confidence to hold her attention.

**C**    over-estimate his listeners' language awareness.

6    They agree that the most effective part of the presentation focused on

**A**    how demotivating an inappropriate approach can be.

**B**    examples of mistakes the presenter had made himself.

**C**    ideas for how to start learning a completely new language.

You will hear a student called Adam Berrington giving a class presentation about a week he spent doing work experience on an alpaca farm. For questions **7 – 14,** complete the sentences with a word or short phrase.

# ALPACA FARM

Adam learnt that the most valuable alpaca wool is the type known as

**(7)** ...............................................

The best alpaca wool tends to be both **(8)** .................................................

in texture and soft to the touch.

A lot of the alpaca wool produced on the farm is sold to **(9)** .................................................

for making into textiles.

Because alpacas are **(10)** .................................................

animals by instinct, alpaca farms need a lot of land.

On his second day, Adam was given the role of **(11)** .................................................

with a group of alpacas.

Maintaining adequate **(12)** .................................................

is one of the main costs facing the alpaca farm.

Adam explains that young alpacas need a shelter to protect them from

**(13)** ................................................. .

Adam uses the word **(14)** .................................................

to summarise the essential character of the alpaca.

**TIP STRIP**

Question 7: Be careful. Two types of wool are mentioned, but only one of them fits here.

Question 8: Listen for the phrase *to get the best price* – the answer comes soon after it.

Question 11: Listen for what the people organising the programme called the role.

Question 14: Adam mentions three adjectives that describe alpacas, but only one of them matches his opinion.

You will hear an interview in which two novelists called Davina Palmer and Dale Kingstone are talking about their careers. For questions **15 – 20**, choose the answer (**A, B C** or **D**) which fits best according to what you hear.

15  Davina says that the success of her first novel

   **A**    came as a complete surprise to her.
   **B**    allowed her to give up her regular job.
   **C**    made it hard for her to plan her future effectively.
   **D**    led to an unexpectedly generous offer of further work.

16  Dale feels that his position as a debut novelist is unlike Davina's for reasons that

   **A**    relate to the type of fiction he writes.
   **B**    arise from the state of the market for fiction.
   **C**    reflect his interest in breaking into other media.
   **D**    result from the greater level of risk that he intends taking.

17  Looking back at her first novel to be translated, Davina regrets

   **A**    not having the confidence to do the work herself.
   **B**    not insisting that her comments were taken seriously.
   **C**    not respecting the experience of her French colleague.
   **D**    not taking more of an interest in all the languages involved.

18  Davina puts her continuing success as a novelist down to her ability to

   **A**    find inspiration in unpromising topics.
   **B**    write to particularly demanding deadlines.
   **C**    draw on her own experiences in her later books.
   **D**    learn from the mistakes made in her early books.

19  Davina tells the story of her book that was rejected to underline

   **A**    the advantages of changing publishers regularly.
   **B**    the dangers of becoming complacent in the face of success.
   **C**    the importance of recognising weaknesses in your own work.
   **D**    the need to find somebody able to provide constructive criticism.

20  When asked about their readers, Dale and Davina both stress the need to

   **A**    keep exploring new ideas in their fiction.
   **B**    accept that not everyone will like their writing.
   **C**    recognise the characteristics of their typical reader.
   **D**    avoid assuming too much about the composition of their readership.

**TIP STRIP**

**Question 16:** Listen for what Dale says about the book industry.

**Question 17:** Listen for how Davina feels now about her behaviour at the time.

**Question 18:** Which option is talking about her whole career?

**Question 20:** You need to listen to what both speakers say in order to answer this question.

You will hear five short extracts in which university students are talking about attending an event called a careers fair.

In the exam, you write your answers **on a separate answer sheet.**

## TASK ONE

For questions **21 – 25**, choose from the list **(A – H)** what most impressed each speaker about the careers fair.

## TASK TWO

For questions **26 – 30**, Choose from the advice each speaker gives about attending career fairs.

**While you listen you must complete both tasks.**

| | | | |
|---|---|---|---|
| A | the physical layout | Speaker 1 | 21 |
| B | the attitude of the organisers | Speaker 2 | 22 |
| C | the range of employers represented | Speaker 3 | 23 |
| D | the chance to meet influential people | Speaker 4 | 24 |
| E | the specific focus of the event | Speaker 5 | 25 |
| F | the practical advice on offer | | |
| G | the material distributed in advance | | |
| H | the opportunity to give feedback | | |

| | | | |
|---|---|---|---|
| A | take key documents with you | Speaker 1 | 26 |
| B | keep a record of new contacts | Speaker 2 | 27 |
| C | pay attention to your appearance | Speaker 3 | 28 |
| D | do plenty of background research | Speaker 4 | 29 |
| E | have realistic expectations | Speaker 5 | 30 |
| F | choose the event itself carefully | | |
| G | plan the day strategically | | |
| H | set yourself ambitious goals | | |

**TIP STRIP**

**Question 21:** Listen for the phrase the *incredible thing was* …. The answer follows this.

**Question 22:** Listen for what surprised the speaker.

**Question 25:** Listen to the second half of what the speaker says to find this answer.

**Question 27:** Listen for when the speaker uses you to give advice to the listener.

# GUIDANCE: SPEAKING

## About the paper

The *Speaking* test lasts for 15 minutes and there are four parts. You take the test with a partner. There are two examiners, although only one (the Interlocutor) speaks to you. You get marks for grammar, vocabulary, discourse management, pronunciation and interactive communication, and these things are assessed throughout the test. You also get a mark for your overall performance.

### Part 1 (2 minutes)

**Testing focus:** You have to show that you can answer social questions in a natural way.

**Procedure:** The Interlocutor asks each of you direct questions in turn on general topics such as your interests, daily routines, likes and dislikes, and what you think about certain issues. You don't interact with your partner in this part.

### Part 2 (4 minutes)

**Testing focus:** You have to demonstrate that you can speak for a minute without support and organise your 'long turn' clearly. You need to compare, describe, give opinions and speculate about two pictures.

**Procedure:** Each of you is given a set of three pictures in turn. You choose two of these pictures to talk about on your own. You compare the pictures you've chosen, and answer two more questions about them. You are also asked a short question about your partner's pictures after they've finished speaking.

### Part 3 (4 minutes)

**Testing focus:** You have a discussion with your partner. You should exchange ideas, express opinions, justify ideas, agree/disagree, give reasons, make suggestions, speculate and negotiate to reach a decision.

**Procedure:** Part 3 is divided into two parts. First, the Interlocutor gives you a task to discuss together for around 2 minutes. There are written prompts with ideas which you can use to support your discussion. The interlocutor then asks you a second question connected to the topic you've been discussing. You have about a minute to try to reach a decision.

### Part 4 (5 minutes)

**Testing focus:** You express and justify opinions, speculate, agree and disagree.

**Procedure:** The Interlocutor asks some questions which broaden the topic of the Part 3 task. Some questions may be addressed to one of you individually, or to both of you together, and in this case it doesn't matter who answers first. Even if your partner is asked a question, you can still add ideas of your own.

## How to do the paper

### Part 1

- **Don't** interact with your partner in this part – the questions will be addressed to each of you in turn. You only need to give short answers about who you are and where you're from.
- When you're asked about more general topics, think of it as being similar to meeting someone in a social situation. You should provide enough detail to be interesting, without using up all the time. Try to be relaxed, and remember it's not what you say that counts, but the way that you say it.

### Part 2

- **Listen** to the Interlocutor's instructions carefully. The task is also written above the pictures to remind you of what to talk about. You can ask the Interlocutor to repeat the task, but only do this if it is really necessary because you risk losing time from your minute.
- It's important to compare the pictures first before moving on to the two questions that form the second part of the task. Don't just describe what's in the pictures, because this won't allow you to show a range of language at the right level. Remember that the second part of the task involves speculation, for example, saying what you think *may, could, might* or *must* be happening.
- Listen to what your partner says when he or she talks about their pictures, because the Interlocutor will ask you a question about them afterwards. In your answer to this question you should give some details, but don't say too much because you only have a short time.

### Part 3

- **Listen** to the task carefully so you understand exactly what you have to do. The task is written on the page with the prompts around it, and you have a short time to read it before you have to start talking. Use this time to check that you understand the question and how each prompt links to it. You can ask the Interlocutor to repeat the task if you're not sure, or check what you have to do with your partner. Once you start, discuss each prompt in turn. Consider the issues in detail, and try to use a range of language.
- It doesn't matter if you don't discuss all the prompts. Make sure you say everything you can about each one before you move on to the next. It's better to discuss those prompts you have ideas about in detail rather than say only a little about each one.
- Give your own opinions, but also ask your partner for his or her views. Really listen to what your partner says so that you can respond to his or her ideas and suggestions appropriately.
- When you're asked to make a decision together, don't make this decision too quickly. You have a minute to discuss it, so continue to use a range of language as you negotiate. There's no 'right' decision, and you're not marked on your opinions, only on your language.

### Part 4

- The Interlocutor may ask a question for both of you to answer, or ask you each a question in turn. You can contribute to your partner's answer, as long as you do this appropriately. The questions in Part 4 are more abstract than those in Part 1, and so you should give longer answers. Try to develop your ideas in an interesting and coherent way, giving examples or reasons for your opinions. You can agree or disagree with what your partner says, and there are no 'right' answers to the questions – you get marks for your language, not your ideas.

## Part 1 (2 minutes)

**The examiner** will ask you a few questions about yourself and what you think about different things.

For example, the examiner might ask you about:

- **area of work or study**
- **general interests**
- **plans and ambitions for the future**
- **experiences of travel**
- **daily life and routines**

### TIP STRIP

**Part 2:**

- **Candidate A:**
Compare two pictures then speculate about the other two questions eg *The people in the market are having fun but if it rained they could move to a shopping mall. The boys need water and sun, so they might be pleased if it rained.*

- **Candidate B,**
you could say: *I think .. would find their situation most problematic because ..*

- **Candidate B:**
Compare two pictures, then speculate about the other two questions eg *The people who are lost need directions, but they don't seem to find the map easy to read. It's hard for the man stuck in snow because anyone coming to help him might get stuck too.*

- **Candidate A,** you could say: *I think they'd all be difficult, but ... would be hardest because ...*

## Part 2 (4 minutes)

**Doing different things**

Turn to the pictures on page 49 which show people doing different things in sunny weather.

*(Candidate A)*:

I'd like you to compare **two** of the pictures and say **why the people might have chosen to do these things in sunny weather, and what difference a change in the weather might make.**

*(Candidate B),* **who do you think would find a change in the weather most problematic? (Why?)**

**Solving problems**

Turn to the pictures on page 50 which show people trying to solve problems.

*(Candidate B),* compare two of the pictures and say **why the people might need to solve these problems, and how easy it might be for them to find the right solution.**

*(Candidate A),* **which of these problems do you think would be the most difficult to solve? (Why?)**

## Part 3 (4 minutes)

Now, I'd like you to talk about something together for about two minutes.

**Here are some things that people often consider when thinking about buying something** and a question for you to discuss. First you have some time to look at the task. *[Turn to the task on page 51]*

Now talk to each other about **how important it is for people to consider these things before buying something.**

Thank you.

Now you have a minute to decide **which is most important for people to consider before buying something as a gift.**

## Part 4 (5 minutes)

*Use the following questions, in order, as appropriate:*

*   **Do you think people buy too many things nowadays? (Why? / Why not?)**

*   **Should we recycle everything instead of buying new items all the time? (Why? / Why not?)**

*   **Some people say shopping is a leisure activity these days. Why do you think this is?**

*   **In your opinion, is advertising a good or a bad thing? (Why?)**

*   **Should children be taught to manage money and budgets at school? (Why? / Why not?)**

*   **Do people have the right priorities in life nowadays? (Why? / Why not?)**

Thank you. That is the end of the test.

| *Select any of the following prompts, as appropriate:* |
| --- |
| *   **What do you think?** |
| *   **Do you agree?** |
| *   **How about you?** |

### TIP STRIP

**Part 3:**

*   It doesn't matter who starts the discussion, but focus on whether these things are important or not and reasons why: *value for money is incredibly important because everyone likes a bargain! On the other hand, if you really want something, it may be worth spending more.*

*   When you're asked to make a decision, don't just repeat what you've said. It's better to talk about new ideas. You don't need to reach a final decision, although it's important to negotiate and try to agree. You could say: *it seems to me that; I'd like to suggest; in my opinion; shall we agree that ... would make a great gift?*

### TIP STRIP

**Part 4:**

Consider the abstract issues behind the questions you could talk about:

*   *too much focus on material possessions, not enough on what's really important in life.*

*   *some things need updating such as technology, but clothes could be recycled.*

*   *people enjoy spending days at a mall with friends – they're not necessarily shopping but it shows how normal shopping has become.*

*   *advertising raises expectations of what people can have and these are often unrealistic.*

*   *one of the most important skills in modern life is being able to look after money, and it's often neglected in schools because they focus on academic subjects.*

*   *it's about balance. People do think about things like taking care of the environment, but media pressure can get in the way. On the whole, I think most people want to live in a good way.*

# PRACTICE TEST 2

## Part 1

For questions **1 – 8**, read the text below and decide which answer (**A, B, C** or **D**) best fits each gap. There is an example at the beginning **(0)**.

In the exam, you mark your answers **on a separate answer sheet**.

**Example:**

**0**    **A** allows          **B** means          **C** gets          **D** makes

| 0 | A | B | C | D |
|---|---|---|---|---|

## Dendrochronology

The science of dendrochronology **(0)** ........... historic buildings to be dated through the examination of the wood used in their construction. As trees grow taller, their trunks get larger in order to **(1)** ........... the increasing weight of branches and leaves. When a tree is cut down, a series of rings can be seen inside the trunk, each **(2)** ........... a year's growth. These rings are most noticeable in temperate regions because they reflect the annual **(3)** ........ of the seasons.

The rings themselves **(4)** ........... us with information about the past. For example a wet year creates a wide ring, **(5)** ........... in a drought year it is narrower. They can also tell us about human activity. Given that a uniform pattern of rings **(6)** ........... in trees of the same species in a particular area, it is possible to **(7)** ........... at the age of an individual tree by analysing its rings.  Whilst it's not always possible to prove that a wooden structure was built in the **(8)** ........ year the wood was felled, it certainly can't be any older than that.

**1**    **A** defend          **B** uphold          **C** support          **D** maintain

**2**    **A** concerning          **B** representing          **C** considering          **D** respecting

**3**    **A** round          **B** lap          **C** turn          **D** cycle

**4**    **A** provide          **B** deliver          **C** produce          **D** reveal

**5**    **A** instead          **B** except          **C** whereas          **D** otherwise

**6**    **A** creates          **B** happens          **C** arises          **D** develops

**7**    **A** calculate          **B** discover          **C** arrive          **D** determine

**8**    **A** correct          **B** exact          **C** definite          **D** true

For questions **9 – 16**, read the text below and think of the word which best fits each gap. Use only one word in each gap. There is an example at the beginning **(0)**.

In the exam, you write your answers **IN CAPITAL LETTERS on a separate answer sheet**.

**Example:** | 0 | | A | S | | | | | | | | | | | | | | | | | | |

## Skiing in the age of global warming

Few sectors of the leisure business are as concerned about the effects of global warming **(0)** ........... the skiing industry. **(9)** ........... weather conditions in ski resorts inevitably vary from year to year, an underlying decline in snowfall levels has been identified. Data provided by leading resorts in the European Alps over a ten-year period shows that average cumulative snowfall – by **(10)** ........... they mean snow that lies on the ground and is good for skiing – has been in marked decline. What's **(11)** ........... , looking back over a 30-year period, the same trend can be identified. In **(12)** ........... words, compared to 30 years ago, all these resorts are now getting much less snow of the type that supports skiing activities.

So **(13)** ........... , the effects on the industry haven't been dramatic – especially at high altitudes, **(14)** ........... good management practices have allowed the slopes to stay open and functioning **(15)** ........... the weather. At lower altitudes, however, the effects are more apparent. A shorter season and increased disruption to bookings can result **(16)** ........ falling profits and threaten the viability of resorts.

## Part 3

For questions **17 – 24**, read the text below. Use the word given in capitals at the end of some of the lines to form a word that fits in the gap **in the same line**. There is an example at the beginning **(0)**.

In the exam, you have to write your answers in **CAPITAL LETTERS on a separate answer sheet**.

**Example:** | 0 | E | S | S | E | N | T | I | A | L | | | | | | | | | | |

---

# Brainpower

In terms of memory, the human brain performs three **(0)** ...........          **ESSENCE**

functions. Firstly, incoming information is understood and recorded

with a high degree of **(17)** ........... . This information is then stored in          **ACCURATE**

a logical way so that it can be retrieved when needed. Finally, a kind

of search engine calls up memories in **(18)** ........... to certain cues. For          **RESPOND**

example, a person's face instantly brings a name to mind, and this is

**(19)** ........... by further details such as occupation, marital status, etc.          **COMPANY**

that allow us to interact **(20)** ........... with them.          **EFFECT**

It's a complex process and inevitably our brains let us down sometimes.

For example, information can be **(21)** ........... at the input stage if we're          **INTERPRET**

distracted or if there's a lack of **(22)** ........... in the way it's presented or          **CLEAR**

explained. Information can also be wrongly **(23)** ........... and therefore          **CATEGORY**

misplaced, making it impossible to find again. Finally, the cues may not

be strong enough. Although a face is instantly recognisable, the name

remains **(24)** ........... We know it's in there somewhere, but we can't call          **ELUDE**

it to mind.

For questions **25 – 30**, complete the second sentence so that it has a similar meaning to the first sentence, using the word given. **Do not change the word given.** You must use between **three** and **six** words, including the word given. Here is an example **(0)**.

**Example:**

**0**    Trevor persuaded his sister to enter the competition.

   **TALKED**

   Trevor ............... entering the competition.

The gap can be filled with the words 'talked his sister into', so you write:

**Example:** | 0 | *TALKED HIS SISTER INTO*

In the exam, you write only the missing words **IN CAPITAL LETTERS on a separate answer sheet**.

---

**25**    Do you mind if I give your name as a referee when I apply for jobs?

   **OBJECTION**

   Would you have ............................... giving your name as a referee when I apply for jobs?

**26**    "Don't forget that you agreed to call your boss, Tina." said Freddie.

   **REMINDED**

   Freddie ............................... agreed to call her boss.

**27**    Students who do a work experience placement tend to be offered more job interviews.

   **LIKELY**

   Doing a work experience placement tends ............................... that students will be offered job interviews.

**28**    If Dario hasn't got enough money left, he probably won't be able to travel.

   **RUNS**

   Dario will probably be able to travel ............................... money.

**29**    Ben fully intends to complete the marathon, despite his recent injury.

   **EVERY**

   Despite his recent injury, Ben ............................... the marathon.

**30**    When Gina started reading Harry's novel, she was very impressed.

   **INITIAL**

   Harry's novel ............................... on Gina

## Part 5

You are going to read a review of two novels featuring twins. For questions **31 – 36**, choose the answer (**A**, **B**, **C** or **D**) which you think fits best according to the text.

In the exam, you mark your answers **on a separate answer sheet**.

# Twin tales

Debra Garth discusses two recent novels featuring twins.

Identical and near-identical twins recur in fiction down through the centuries. As well as providing plenty of mileage for plot lines involving impersonation and mistaken identity, they can give a twist to any traditional story. The possibilities appear endless. In the real world, twins are now more common than ever before. Increased use of fertility drugs, a rise in older women giving birth and better prenatal care mean that the number of twins born in Britain and North America since the 1980s has nearly doubled. Despite this, twins, and particularly identicals, remain a subject of fascination for novelists and readers alike.

At the centre of each of two recent books is a set of identical siblings. These works both reflect on a moment that occurs in every life, twin or not, when a child nears adulthood and steps away from the family. In the 19th century, family was a prevailing theme in English literature: the impact of birth was inescapable; an individual's fortunes rose and fell with their kin, and the actions of one family member affected the whole. Now society, and fiction too, is more atomised. Most modern British or American works probe the choices individuals make for themselves. Even modern
line 12 biography often succumbs to this trend, emphasising the personal life of an historic figure, rather than upbringing. The mini-genre of twin-lit exploits the tension between these two ways of seeing the world. The reader is asked to judge to what extent an individual's will or imagination can triumph over their DNA.

Audrey Niffenegger's *Her Fearful Symmetry* delves into this idea through the story of identical twins who jointly inherit their aunt's wordly goods. This young pair, Julia and Valentina, are mirror twins: one is left-handed, the other right. Niffenegger is no stranger to the fantastical storyline, and this book also consciously pays homage to its historic antecedents – the title alludes to a William Blake poem. Yet this is also a modern work about identity. The young twins move into their aunt's flat when they turn 21. Away from home for the first time, each character develops. In a progression familiar from other twin novels, the two gradually pull apart.

The tensions arising out of the sisters' close bond provide the best moments in this book. "I wish I could leave her," Valentina says of Julia. Her boyfriend replies: "You're not married to her. You can do what you like." But he's not a twin; he doesn't understand. Can you be with another person and really be yourself? This question is at the heart of the book. *Her Fearful Symmetry* crafts the early stages of crisis well but, as it progresses, it commits the ultimate sin for a twin novel: it fails to distinguish between two identicals. And part-way through, the narrative suddenly shifts from a story about family to an increasingly erratic plot about the dead aunt. The novel implicitly explores whether it's possible to escape one's family – can the self exist without its shapers? Its answer is emphatically, and tragically, 'no'.

The idea recurs, to better effect, in Diana Evans' debut novel entitled simply *26a*. This is the story of Georgia and Bessi, born 45 minutes apart. Like *Her Fearful Symmetry*, *26a* touches on the ideas we voyeuristically expect of identicals: the extraordinary closeness and similarities in the childhood selves. When the twins are put in different school classes, "it felt like being halved and doubled at the same time".

But the move towards self-recognition is both sharp and poignant, perhaps because Evans herself was born a twin. She's lived with the question of oneness in twoness her whole life. Early in *26a*, Georgia says of her twin: "She's the best bit of me. We're half each." And this innocent notion plays out to a heartbreaking conclusion. The brilliance of this novel is to make us love each twin and see both sides: we seek both the comfort of Georgia loving Bessi, yet feel Bessi's desperation to escape twindom and find her own path. This is pure, unsentimental love of the clearest kind; the result is one of the few novels I've cried at even on second reading.

The two novels have surprising similarities, particularly with regard to love. Both conclude that platonic love between siblings can be as glorious, as troubling and as crushing as any other kind. By analysing this idea through twins, however, there's a further question: whether a sense of self can be maintained when the bond is so close. A French aphorism famously recounts that, in love, there's always a lover and a loved one. Is equality possible in any loving relationship? Evans and Niffenegger both conclude not. And, as any old-fashioned novel will affirm, it is loving, not being loved, that causes problems.

**31**  In the first paragraph, the reviewer points out that twins

  **A**    are now better understood than in the past.

  **B**    often feature in rather predictable literary plots.

  **C**    are now more prevalent in real life than in fiction.

  **D**    continue to provide a source of inspiration for writers.

**32**  What is the reviewer referring to in the phrase 'this trend' in line 12?

  **A**    The inevitable weakening of family ties in adulthood.

  **B**    A tendency to downplay the importance of family background.

  **C**    The pressure on individuals to conform to certain family expectations.

  **D**    A desire to read about the private lives of people from famous families.

**33**  What is suggested about the author of *Her Fearful Symmetry* in the third paragraph?

  **A**    She is trying to look at twins in a new way.

  **B**    She doesn't usually write books of this type.

  **C**    She wants the book to fit into a literary tradition.

  **D**    She is hoping to bring a genre of writing up to date.

**34**  What is the reviewer's main criticism of *Her Fearful Symmetry?*

  **A**    The story loses its sense of direction.

  **B**    It reaches a rather negative conclusion.

  **C**    Its central theme is insufficiently developed.

  **D**    The characters are not drawn clearly enough.

**35**  For the reviewer, the emotional power of the novel *26a* stems from

  **A**    the author's first-hand knowledge of her subject.

  **B**    the way it deals with our assumptions about twins.

  **C**    the simple language used to express complex ideas.

  **D**    the reader having to identify with one of the two characters.

**36**  The reviewer concludes that both novels describe a relationship between twins that

  **A**    generates fewer problems than other similar situations.

  **B**    has parallels with those between romantic couples.

  **C**    is quite unlike those found in other family contexts.

  **D**    is similar to that explored by traditional fiction.

## Part 6

You are going to read four extracts from articles about an art exhibition For questions **37 – 40**, choose from the art critics **A – D**. The art critics may be chosen more than once.

In the exam, you mark your answers on **a separate answer sheet**.

### Critic A

Few artists have such a melodramatic biography as the Italian painter Caravaggio (1571–1610). A dissolute hot-tempered man, he was often embroiled in scandal. Yet, this prodigious artist changed the course of European art. It is this dualism that makes him a figure of perpetual fascination, and explains why Londoners and tourists alike have flocked to see the exhibition *Beyond Caravaggio* at the National Gallery. This sets out to show how painters all over Europe became obsessed with his innovations, seeking to incorporate them into their own work. The trouble is, too often, the product of a second-rate artist attempting to 'do' a Caravaggio is disappointing and too many of those featured alongside Caravaggio fall a long way short of his exacting standards. What's more, the distribution of his work through the exhibition is rather uneven: two of the six being co-located in one space, whilst other rooms have none at all. Although there's also a film to see in which the great man's influence is discussed by leading academics, this feels like an afterthought and doesn't make up for the shortcomings of the exhibition itself.

### Critic B

Stick the name Caravaggio in the title of an exhibition, and you can guarantee queues round the block. He seems more like the antihero of a potboiler than a man of flesh and blood. Make no mistake, though: *Beyond Caravaggio* at the National Gallery isn't just a monographic show devoted to this charismatic Italian, who revolutionised art by painting directly from life and experimenting with dramatic effects of lighting. Rather, it's about something subtler: Caravaggio's impact on his immediate circle and followers, and it's been very imaginatively put together in a series of interconnected rooms. Indeed, of the 49 breathtaking paintings in the exhibition, only six are by Caravaggio himself. The rest are by accomplished painters from all over Europe; testimony to just how far his influence extended. An absorbing video accompanies the exhibition – informative and accessible, it really helped me grasp why painting owes such a debt to this great man.

### Critic C

If, like countless others, you're enticed to visit this exhibition, intrigued to see at first hand the gloriously lifelike masterworks of the man who changed the course of art history, you'd better steel yourself for a disappointment. The show begins, at least, with two bona fide Caravaggios: an early picture of a boy peeling fruit, from 1592–93 and *Boy Bitten by a Lizard* (1594–95). These are joined by two imposing paintings by Caravaggio's assistant Cecco. The rest of the offering is unfortunately rather lacklustre in comparison. If we need to see Caravaggio's work alongside the work of lesser painters in order to appreciate his greatness, there should at least be one of his paintings in each room. By the time you reach the end, the focus on Caravaggio is quite lost. An informative, if rather dull, video concludes the tour, but you're not exactly encouraged to watch it. I expect many visitors don't even realise it's there.

### Critic D

Most people have heard the name Caravaggio and have an idea of the colourful reputation enjoyed by the 16th-century Italian artist. So in terms of visitor numbers, it was a shrewd move by the National Gallery to use his name in the title even though only six of the paintings on show are by the man himself. But these are cleverly juxtaposed as you move from room to room. Seeing works by the master and his imitators in close proximity, you're left in no doubt as to exactly where the originality and genius lay. After a while, though, you grow tired of the poor imitations, and head back to see the work of the great man himself. I found the film an invaluable adjunct to the exhibition. For anyone without training in art history, it makes all the connections very eloquently.

**Which art critic**

has a similar view to Critic A regarding the way the exhibition has been laid out?

**37** ☐

has a different view to Critic D regarding the quality of the majority of the paintings on show?

**38** ☐

holds a similar view to Critic B about the effectiveness of the video that accompanies the exhibition?

**39** ☐

has a different opinion to the others about why so many people have been to see the exhibition?

**40** ☐

## Part 7

You are going to read an article about studying economics. Six paragraphs have been removed from the article. Choose from the paragraphs **A – G** the one which fits each gap (**41 – 46**). There is one extra paragraph you do not need to use.

In the exam, you mark your answers **on a separate answer sheet**.

## Crash and learn

*How the financial crisis of 2008 changed the study of economics*

It was November 2012 when seven undergraduates met in a cramped room on the top floor of Manchester university's student union. Chairs drawn into a semi-circle, they listened as two founding members of the Post-Crash Economics Society went through a brief PowerPoint presentation explaining what they thought was wrong with the economics curriculum. A polite discussion followed before everyone shuffled off for the winter holidays. Although hardly a momentous event in itself, it was part of something much bigger. The gathering had taken place in response to an email with the subject line: "Call out to all the Econosceptics out there".

**41**

Picking up on this line of questioning, the presenters asked: "How far can economics be called a real science?" This was an allusion to academic economists' tendency to present their equations and mathematical identities as iron laws rather than imperfect attempts to model unpredictable human interactions. Isn't economics, they suggested, really more like politics than physics?

**42**

In 2011, students there had set up a Society for Economic Pluralism, galvanised by attending a corporate-sponsored party at which attendees seemed only to want to talk about getting jobs in the financial sector. It was, says PhD student and co-founder Rafe Martyn, aimed at those "who learn economics to make the world a better place rather than just improve their private-sector employability".

**43**

The experts who were thought to have solved, once and for all, the problems of economic boom and slump, and who had ignored – even celebrated – widening inequality in most advanced countries, were now coming under fire. This was because they'd proved completely lacking in their powers of prediction and remedy.

**44**

The most glaring shortcoming of such theoretical constructs, students argued, was the failure to provide an explanation for the recent financial crash itself. The subject wasn't even mentioned in many first-year undergraduate courses in 2011. Rather, the lecturers appeared to believe in an economic system that was largely self-correcting; one that would return naturally to a state of equilibrium.

**45**

Even so, against the odds, the students' protests gained momentum and began to nudge change. By 2016, several universities in Britain were offering courses that approached economics with a wider perspective. Second-year students at Cambridge, for example, were able to take a 30-lecture course on the History and Philosophy of Economics, in what was the first such programme at a major English-speaking university in a generation. At Manchester, too, broader-based modules were being introduced, too late and too narrow for the students who pushed for change back in 2012, but a breakthrough nonetheless.

**46**

Today's students are, after all, tomorrow's trained economists, who will be running economies from their desks in government, banks, multilateral institutions and think tanks. What students learn about how economies work and how governments can influence outcomes will have a profound impact on future policies covering everything from tax and spending to interest rates, minimum wages, greenhouse-gas emissions and trade.

**A** Despite this fall from grace, they continued to put faith in elegant economic models. These presented an explanation of human behaviour in which individuals and institutions were assumed to make rational decisions in their own economic interest, within certain societal and legal constraints.

**B** "It did all start happening," insists Diane Coyle, professor of economics at Manchester University. "Almost anybody teaching economics came to accept that, post-crash, the curriculum needed reforming, though I understand why for students this may all have seemed impossibly slow."

**C** "In the middle of the biggest global recession for 80 years," it read, "students across the world are questioning the very foundations of our discipline." It asked whether the economics they were learning, dominated by mathematical formula and abstract models, was relevant to the real world.

**D** Meanwhile, the society that had kickstarted it all hadn't stood still either. It had evolved into Rethinking Economics, a charity that linked more than 40 student groups pressing for curriculum changes in campuses across the world. It had become a force for change that had implications far beyond academia.

**E** Similar groups began to take root on other campuses, Manchester amongst them, as it became apparent that the financial crash was going to provoke political upheavals across Europe and North America, and this was putting profound pressure on the economics profession.

**F** Their students found this argument unsatisfactory. They felt they were being taught the methodology of a pseudoscience, which was based on a largely discredited set of assumptions. Initially, however, their complaints were met by the determination of many in the economic establishment to defend their turf.

**G** They weren't alone in voicing such doubts about this rigidity in the prevailing approach. Ha-Joon Chang, a developmental economist who teaches at the University of Cambridge, remembers students banging on the door, saying, "There's the biggest financial crisis since 1929 going on around us and our professors teach as if nothing has happened."

## Part 8

You are going to read an article about the design of chairs. For questions **47 – 56**, choose from the designers (**A – D**). The designers may be chosen more than once.

In the exam, you mark your answers **on a separate answer sheet**.

**Which designer mentions**

| | |
|---|---|
| chairs becoming the focus of disagreements? | 47 |
| a chair which it took time to develop fully? | 48 |
| chairs providing evidence of changing ideas about design over time? | 49 |
| an explanation for the way people feel about chairs? | 50 |
| a chair that might represent good value for an art collector? | 51 |
| a chair that seems to sum up the spirit of an era? | 52 |
| why the idea of the chair continues to attract the attention of designers? | 53 |
| a famous chair that wasn't quite what it seemed? | 54 |
| a chair which is a surprisingly modern in appearance? | 55 |
| the source of inspiration for the use of one material in chair-making? | 56 |

# The art of the chair

Four leading designers talk about the simple household object.

**A Ben Levenstein**

Before the digital revolution changed everything, it used to be possible to tell the story of design through a sequence of chairs. They could take you from the start of mass production, when the Thonet family set up their first factory in the beech forests of central Europe, to the most recent experiments in blow-moulded plastic. Between the two, every movement in architecture and design has left its mark. You might not want to sit in it, but Gerrit Rietveld's Red Blue chair says as much about the aesthetics of the early 20th century as a painting by Piet Mondrian, and you can own a version for a lot less. At the Bauhaus school in Germany, Marcel Breuer saw the creative possibilities of tubular steel. The story goes that, while cycling, he looked down at his handlebars and realised that the same substance could be used for furniture. The result was the Wassily armchair, designed for his friend, the painter Wassily Kandinsky, who was also teaching at the school.

**B Susan Candler**

There are, of course, countless four-legged chairs but almost as many three-legged ones, cantilevered ones, and chairs on wheels. There are chairs made of wood, steel, aluminium, cardboard, glass and plastic in every permutation. There are chairs designed to be comfortable, and chairs designed to look comfortable. There are chairs to sit in, and chairs to hang your jacket on. There are chairs that sell at auction for the price of a major work of art, and there are disposable chairs. For me, Charles and Ray Eames' Lounge chair serves to define modern splendour. It was designed over a protracted period in the 1950s through a process of refining timber-moulding techniques and developing a rubber mounting that gave the chair enough yield to make it comfortable. But while a car or a refrigerator from the same moment has turned into a period piece, the Eames' work looks as if it still belongs to the present. Robin Day was responsible for the cheap, tough and stylish Polyprop chair that epitomises everything that was optimistic about Britain in the 1960s.

**C Evie Lambett**

Sceptics claim that the world has no need for yet another designer to design yet another chair. But even if design is no longer only about physical objects, people in the profession go on creating chairs. What's more, unlike almost any other piece of domestic equipment, you don't just buy chairs, you collect them. Peter Smithson, one of the more sophisticated British architects of the 1960s, who designed the suave *Economist* building on St. James's Street, believed it was because they looked cute. "It is probable that we see them as domestic pets – they have legs, feet, arms, and backs," he wrote. "They are symmetrical in one direction, like animals, or like ourselves. The act of marking territory starts with our clothes, with our style, with our gestures and postures when we wear them. With a chair we extend our sense of territory beyond our skin."

**D Ray Harrison**

It's not hard to see the appeal of a chair to a designer: they make them famous and if they're good, they don't date. Chairs last for much longer than laptops or washing machines, and not just physically; the idea behind a chair stays relevant too. If chairs have become collectors' pieces, they've also become the subject of acrimonious litigation about what's genuine, and what's not – a difficult concept when applied to objects that were intended to be mass-produced. English model Christine Keeler made Arne Jacobsen's curvaceous plywood Ant chair famous when she was photographed sitting on one in 1963. Except that it was a fake. Jacobsen's original version doesn't have a slot in the back. Alvar Aalto, the architect who was enough of a national hero in Finland to appear on a banknote, designed a simple stool with bent plywood legs. Ikea does a version that's far cheaper, but put the two versions together and you won't mistake the genuine article. For the rest of us, we go on sitting in them, using them to say something about the look of our homes, and who we think we are.

You **must** answer this question. Write your answer in **220 – 260** words in an appropriate style.

In the exam, you write your answer **on a separate answer sheet**.

---

1 Your class has recently watched a TV discussion on whether technology has really improved the quality of our lives. You have made the notes below:

<u>**Has technology really improved the quality of our lives?**</u>

- saves time

- costs money

- creates dependency

Some opinions expressed in the discussion:

"It saves time when it works, but can take a long time to fix."

"Having the latest technology is often expensive and it needs upgrading very quickly."

"It makes people dependent on it, and they can't manage without it."

Write an essay discussing **two** of the points in your notes. You should **explain whether technology has really improved the quality of our lives**, **giving reasons** in support of your answer.

You may, if you wish, make use of the opinions expressed in the discussion, but you should use your own words as far as possible.

Write an answer to **one** of the questions **2 – 4** in this part. Write your answer in **220 – 260** words in an appropriate style.

In the exam, you write your answer on **a separate answer sheet**. Put the question number in the box at the top of the answer sheet.

2   You have returned from an exchange visit to a college in another country. Now your principal has asked you to write a report about your experience. In your report you should explain what happened during the visit, consider the value of the whole trip, and recommend any changes that might improve the experience for students in the future.

Write your **report**.

3   You see the following announcement in a nature magazine.

> Do you do anything to help your local environment? Do you think individuals can really make a difference?
>
> Send us a letter about your experiences, outlining what you do and explaining why you think it is important. We will publish the best letters in the magazine.

Write your **letter**.

4   You read the following advertisement in an in-flight magazine.

> # Can you write a good review?
>
> We're planning a series of reviews about films people enjoy watching on a long journey, to include in our in-flight magazine.
>
> Send us a review of a film you have watched on a long journey. Was it absorbing enough to pass the time? Did you learn anything from watching it? Was it memorable?

Write your **review**.

# Part 1

You will hear three different extracts. For questions **1 – 6**, choose the answer (**A, B** or **C**) which fits best according to what you hear. There are two questions for each extract.

In the exam, you write your answers **on a separate answer sheet**.

## Extract One

You will hear two film critics talking about a new movie.

1    What do they agree about it?

    **A**    The plot lacks pace.
    **B**    The music is rather sentimental in places.
    **C**    The lead actor lacks the maturity to play the role credibly.

2    In the man's opinion, it is a mistake to

    **A**    compare the movie with others by the same director.
    **B**    judge the movie by the standards set by larger studios.
    **C**    see the movie as part of a recent trend amongst filmmakers.

## Extract Two

You hear two students talking about their rented apartments.

3    When the girl found previous tenants' possessions in her apartment, she felt

    **A**    amused at her first reaction to them.
    **B**    annoyed by the carelessness of others.
    **C**    unsettled by what they made her think.

4    Why did the man open the letter from a lawyer?

    **A**    He wanted to check that it wasn't important.
    **B**    He realised he should return it to the sender.
    **C**    He was intrigued to find out what it was about.

## Extract Three

You hear part of an interview with an environmentalist.

5    In her view, the report into the sale of public woodlands

    **A**    tended to make rather unreal distinctions.
    **B**    should have come to a more definite conclusion.
    **C**    provided a relatively balanced discussion of the issues.

6    She suggests that quotes from the report in the media

    **A**    have contained some inaccuracies.
    **B**    have been used to misrepresent its findings.
    **C**    have been widely misunderstood by the public.

You will hear a student giving a presentation about a musical instrument maker called Terje Isungset. For questions **7 – 14**, complete the sentences with a word or short phrase.

In the exam, you write your answers **on a separate answer sheet**.

# TERJE ISUNGSET: MAKING MUSIC OUT OF ICE

Terje feels that his experience as a **(7)** ................................................

musician has helped his creativity.

Terje uses the word **(8)** ...................................................

to describe the sort of music he felt dissatisfied playing.

The idea of making instruments out of ice came to Terje at a

**(9)** ................................................. where a concert was going to be held.

The speaker particularly likes the sound of the instruments called

**(10)** ................................................. , which Terje plays.

Terje ran into problems when he recorded an album in a

**(11)** ................................................. inside a glacier.

In the initial stages of making an instrument, Terje uses

**(12)** ................................................. and saws as tools.

Terje insists that **(13)** ...................................................

ice doesn't make instruments with a good sound.

When Terje gives a concert, **(14)** .................................................

is the thing most likely to prevent him playing.

You will hear an interview with a brother and sister called Simon and Dawn Drayton, who run a large window-cleaning company. For questions **15 – 20**, choose the answer (**A, B, C** or **D**) which fits best according to what you hear.

In the exam, you write your answers **on a separate answer sheet**.

15 Dawn feels that she and Simon signed up their first clients as a result of

    **A**    the quality of their work.

    **B**    word-of-mouth recommendations.

    **C**    the positive initial impression they made.

    **D**    being introduced to them by a reliable colleague.

16 What does Simon say about their investment in setting up the business?

    **A**    He regrets borrowing money to buy a van.

    **B**    He accepts that they made some bad choices.

    **C**    He recognises that a sacrifice he made paid off.

    **D**    He's grateful for the financial support of his family.

17 Dawn explains that the company grew so fast because they

    **A**    saw a way of offering big clients a more efficient service.

    **B**    joined forces with other similar companies in their area.

    **C**    targeted the particular needs of clients in the retail sector.

    **D**    continued to have both domestic and commercial clients.

18 Simon left the company for a while because he

    **A**    took an opportunity to sell part of the business.

    **B**    thought that Dawn would manage it better alone.

    **C**    disagreed with Dawn about how it should be run.

    **D**    felt the need for a more reliable source of income.

19 Dawn was unsure about Simon rejoining the company because

    **A**    she didn't want it to grow any further.

    **B**    she wasn't convinced it was the best thing for him.

    **C**    she feared that their previous problems would return.

    **D**    she didn't want to change the way things were organised.

20 Simon and Dawn both feel that the success of their company is based on

    **A**    the attitude it has towards its employees.

    **B**    the closeness of their personal relationship.

    **C**    the cooperative feeling amongst the managers.

    **D**    the positive profile it has in the wider community.

# Part 4

You will hear five short extracts in which people are talking about language courses they are doing.

In the exam, you write your answers **on a separate answer sheet.**

## TASK ONE

For questions **21 – 25**, choose from the list (**A – H**) what led each speaker to attend the language course.

## TASK TWO

For questions **26 – 30**, choose from list (**A – H**) what each speaker has found surprising about the course.

**While you listen you must complete both tasks.**

| | |
|---|---|
| **A** a desire to travel | **A** the attitude of classmates |
| **B** an interest in the culture | **B** the facilities at the venue |
| **C** the suggestion of a friend | **C** the teaching methods |
| **D** an online review | **D** the range of skills practised |
| **E** some available funds | **E** the topics discussed |
| **F** some persuasive publicity | **F** the insistence on accuracy |
| **G** a wish to support another person | **G** the speed of progress |
| **H** wanting better employment prospects | **H** the amount of homework |

| | |
|---|---|
| Speaker 1 | 21 |
| Speaker 2 | 22 |
| Speaker 3 | 23 |
| Speaker 4 | 24 |
| Speaker 5 | 25 |

| | |
|---|---|
| Speaker 1 | 26 |
| Speaker 2 | 27 |
| Speaker 3 | 28 |
| Speaker 4 | 29 |
| Speaker 5 | 30 |

## Part 1 (2 minutes)

**The examiner** will ask you a few questions about yourself and what you think about different things.

- **area of work or study**
- **general interests**
- **plans and ambitions for the future**
- **experiences of travel**
- **daily life and routines**

## Part 2 (4 minutes)

Turn to the pictures on page 52 which show **people spending time in a forest**.

**Ways of spending time**

*(Candidate A)*, compare two of the pictures and say **why the people might have chosen to spend time in the forest and how enjoyable the experience might be**.

*(Candidate B)*, **which of these experiences do you think would be least enjoyable. Why?**

**Looking at things**

Turn to the pictures on page 54 which show **people looking at things in different situations**.

*(Candidate B)*, compare two of the pictures and say **why the people might be looking at these things and how they might be feeling**.

*(Candidate A)*, **who do you think will remember what they've seen the longest? Why?**

## Part 3 (4 minutes)

**How technology affects our lives**

Turn to the task on page 53.

Talk to each other about **whether the ways in which technology affects our lives are positive or negative**.

Now decide **which effect has changed most people's lives for the better**.

## Part 4 (5 minutes)

Answer the following questions in order, as appropriate:

- **Some people dislike using any form of technology. Why do you think this is?**
- **Why do you think social networking sites are so popular?**
- **In your opinion, when should children be allowed to have a phone? (Why?)**
- **Do you think that computers really save time? (Why? / Why not?)**
- **Some people say technology causes more problems than it solves. What do you think?**
- **Is there any technology you think would be difficult to live without? (Why?)**

# ISUALS BANK

## Part 2 Student A

- Why might the people have chosen to do these things in sunny weather?
- What difference might a change in the weather make?

**Part 2** Student B

- Why might the people need to solve these problems?

- How easy might it be for them to find the right solution?

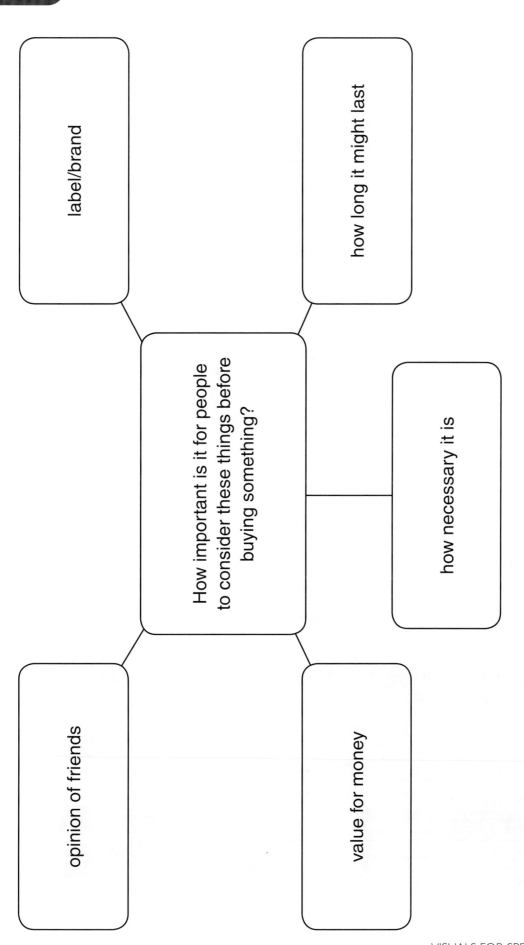

label/brand

how long it might last

How important is it for people
to consider these things before
buying something?

how necessary it is

opinion of friends

value for money

**Part 2** Student A

- Why might the people have chosen to spend time in the forest?

- How enjoyable might their experience be?

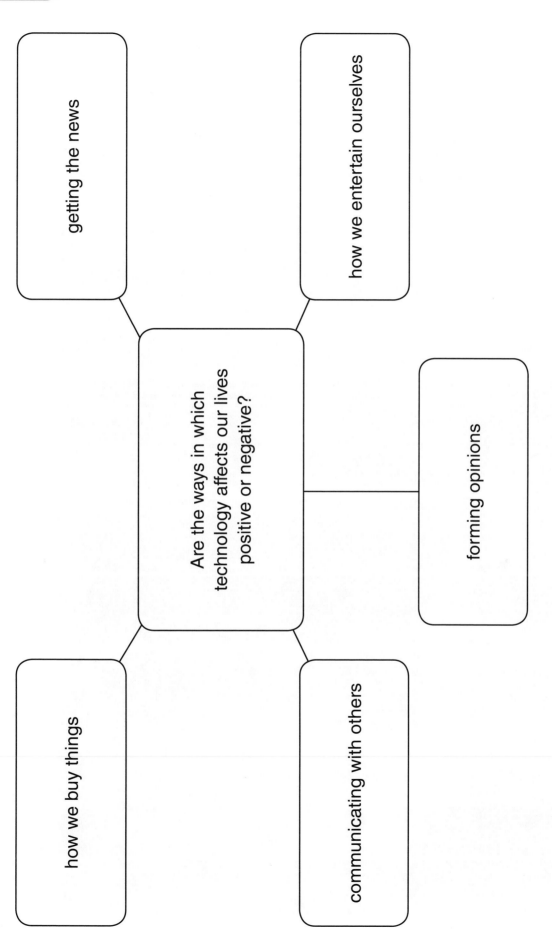

getting the news

how we entertain ourselves

Are the ways in which technology affects our lives positive or negative?

forming opinions

how we buy things

communicating with others

- Why might the people be looking at these things?

- How might they be feeling?

# SPEAKING BANK

## Part 1

In Part 1, you answer questions about yourself from the examiner (for two minutes) on personal topics such as your likes and dislikes, everyday life and routines, work, study, holiday preferences and so on. Do not discuss them with your partner.

### Exam help

- ✓ These are normal social questions, so reply confidently and in an interesting way. Don't just answer 'yes' or 'no', or mumble.
- ✓ Try to extend vocabulary around the topic by giving examples.
- ✓ Think about the tense of the question. Do you need to answer in the past, the present or the future?

### Useful language

**Communicative strategies**
So do you mean … ?
Could you say that again, please?
Sorry, I didn't quite catch that.
Well, that depends on …
That's a really interesting question.
Oh, yes, absolutely/very much so.
No, I'm afraid I don't.
Definitely!
Well, how can I put this?

**Giving personal information**
I enjoy … That's why I …
I've always (dis)liked … because …
To be honest, I'm not very good at …

My favourite things are …
I guess I'm a … because …
What I've always preferred is …

**Responding to social questions**
Although I love …, I don't do much … because …
I haven't finally decided …, but I'd probably like to …
I used to be keen on …, but now …
I honestly don't like … very much, though I do enjoy …
The last time I … was …
I've never … though I'd like to try.
I'm still thinking about … but at the moment I …

## Part 2

In Part 2, you compare two pictures form a choice of three and say something else about them. You speak on your own for about a minute. After you've spoken your partner will be asked a short question on the topic of your pictures.

### Exam help

- ✓ There are three parts to the task – comparing the pictures and answering two further questions. Start by comparing the people, places and situations in the two pictures you choose. Don't just describe the pictures, as you won't use C1 level language.
- ✓ Don't stop if you can't remember a word or what something is called.
- ✓ Use varied vocabulary and complex language.
- ✓ It's better if you're still talking at the end of the minute so that the examiner stops you. Even if there's still time left when you've said everything you want to, **don't** talk about the third picture.

### Useful language

**Comparing the pictures**
Both the pictures show people … but they're in different places.
In the first picture they're …, whereas in the second …
These are very different ways of …
I can see some similarities between the pictures – like the people seem to be friends …
There are several differences between the pictures. First, …
The first picture looks busier than the second because …
The boy in the cinema is enjoying himself more than …
There's a big difference between these two pictures. One is … but the other …
The first picture is outside, whereas the second one is inside.

**Speculating and answering the questions**
I'm not entirely sure, but I think they're probably …
I can't see exactly what they're doing, but it could be …
Perhaps they've decided to do this because …
The boy in the first picture seems to be …
The girl looks like she's about to …
He may have chosen to be there because …
All the people are probably …
I think the girl may be feeling … because …
If they don't … they might …
What will probably happen is …
The result could be …

In Part 3, you discuss a task with your partner. You're given a question with 5 written prompts to talk about. You discuss these prompts in as much detail as you can, putting forward ideas and responding appropriately to each other's comments. After two minutes the examiner will stop you and give you another related question to discuss and reach a decision on.

## Exam help

- ✓ Focus on the task – the question is printed in the central box. You don't need to talk about all the prompts, so if you don't have any ideas about one of them, move on to the next. You can also add your own ideas. What's important is that you use language at the right level, not how many prompts you can mention in two minutes.
- ✓ If your partner doesn't say much, involve him/her in the discussion by asking his/her opinions. You'll be given credit for that. When your partner gives an opinion, respond fully to what they've said before moving onto something else. This shows that you're genuinely listening and interacting
- ✓ After your two-minute discussion, you'll be given another question connected to the task, and asked to reach a decision. You have a minute for this, so don't make your decision too quickly, but give reasons for your choice. You can choose prompts you've already discussed, or prompts you didn't have time for.

## Useful language

### Asking your partner for their opinion and interacting with them

I don't think … would work. Do you?
Some of these ideas don't seem useful.
What do you think?
I don't know about you, but in my opinion …
You may disagree with me, but I think …
You probably don't think the same as me, but …
What do you think? Is this a better idea?
You said … Can you explain what you mean?
You seem to think … Is that right?
Why do you think that's a good choice?

### Justifying your ideas and responding to your partner's opinions

I understand what you're saying, …
I'm sure most people would agree with you, though …
In spite of what you've said, in my opinion, …
That's an interesting point of view, but maybe we need to consider …
If I understood you correctly, you said …
That's a valuable comment, but don't you think it might useful to … ?
As you said, … However, have you thought about …
I take your point, but I still think …
I'm afraid I don't agree. I really believe that …
I really like what you said about … and I'd like to add …
I love your idea about … because …

### Moving from one written prompt to another

So why don't we discuss … ?
Do you have anything to say about this?
We haven't talked about … yet.
Shall we discuss the idea of … next?
We've probably said enough about … , don't you think? Let's move on.
We've said enough about that point – why don't we consider …
That seems to bring us on to …

In Part 4, you discuss abstract questions from the examiner related to the topic you discussed in Part 3. These questions ask for your opinions, and you should give more detailed answers than you did in Part 1. The examiner may ask you a question directly, or to both of you. In either case you can respond to what your partner says by agreeing, disagreeing or adding more information. The examiner won't join in your discussion.

## Exam help

✓ Give extended answers including reasons and examples for your ideas, and use complex language if possible. The examiner wants to hear what you can do, so don't just give simple answers.

✓ Remember, you can interact with your partner even if the question wasn't addressed to you initially. Part 4 is a discussion, which allows you to develop ideas and share opinions.

✓ Don't be afraid to talk about your opinions or feelings. There are no 'correct' answers to any of the questions. You're not being assessed on your opinions, but do give reasons or examples to back up your ideas.

## Useful language

### Giving opinions

I've never really thought about that before, but …
Personally, I feel strongly that …
I don't think anyone should …
It seems unlikely that anybody would …
People often say that … , but I …
I think people find it really difficult to …
I'm not sure about … , to be perfectly honest.
Let's think positively and say …
On the whole, I think that …
I've often thought that …

### Giving examples and/or reasons

To make it clear what I mean …
I can think of one example, which is …
I once had an experience that …
Let me explain why …
For example, when anyone …
There are lots of reasons for this …
People are often against this. I think it's because …
I'm still young, and that's why …

### Adding to what your partner has said

I think he/she has made a really good point, and I'd like to add …
I agree with what he/she said, and I'd also like to say …
That's all true, and on top of that …
He/she has mentioned everything I'd have said, but maybe he/she could have included …
What he/she said is right, but it could also be said that …
I think he/she has left out the idea that …
I couldn't have put it better, but I think there's also the point that …

**WRITING BANK**

### Exam question

Your class has attended a debate on whether advertising can have a great influence on young people. You have made the notes below:

> **How does advertising influence young people today?**
> - creates trends
> - raises expectations
> - increases awareness

> Some opinions expressed in the debate:
>
> "It creates trends that make young people feel part of a group."
>
> "It raises unrealistic expectations of what young people can afford."
>
> "It makes young people more aware of what's good and what's bad."

Write an essay discussing **two** of the points in your notes about how advertising can influence young people. You should explain which one you think is most influential giving reasons to support your opinion.

You may, if you wish, make use of the opinions expressed in the debate, but you should use your own words as far as possible.

Write your answer in **220 – 260** words in an appropriate style

### Sample answer

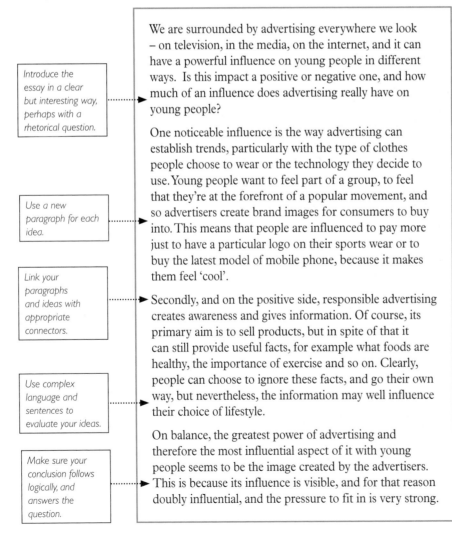

*Introduce the essay in a clear but interesting way, perhaps with a rhetorical question.*

We are surrounded by advertising everywhere we look – on television, in the media, on the internet, and it can have a powerful influence on young people in different ways. Is this impact a positive or negative one, and how much of an influence does advertising really have on young people?

*Use a new paragraph for each idea.*

One noticeable influence is the way advertising can establish trends, particularly with the type of clothes people choose to wear or the technology they decide to use. Young people want to feel part of a group, to feel that they're at the forefront of a popular movement, and so advertisers create brand images for consumers to buy into. This means that people are influenced to pay more just to have a particular logo on their sports wear or to buy the latest model of mobile phone, because it makes them feel 'cool'.

*Link your paragraphs and ideas with appropriate connectors.*

Secondly, and on the positive side, responsible advertising creates awareness and gives information. Of course, its primary aim is to sell products, but in spite of that it can still provide useful facts, for example what foods are healthy, the importance of exercise and so on. Clearly, people can choose to ignore these facts, and go their own way, but nevertheless, the information may well influence their choice of lifestyle.

*Use complex language and sentences to evaluate your ideas.*

*Make sure your conclusion follows logically, and answers the question.*

On balance, the greatest power of advertising and therefore the most influential aspect of it with young people seems to be the image created by the advertisers. This is because its influence is visible, and for that reason doubly influential, and the pressure to fit in is very strong.

### Useful language

**Introduction**

It is often said that …
How much of an effect does it have?
There is no obvious answer as to whether it is …
The question is open to debate …

**Ordering and evaluating ideas**

To start with, …
A further point is …
In addition to this, …
Nevertheless …
On the positive/negative side …
How important is this really … ?
This would seem to indicate that …

**Giving reasons**

This means that …
This could be taken as …
It seems to be because …
For that reason it is …
Clearly, this indicates that …

**Conclusion**

To sum up, I would say that …
Having considered all the arguments, I believe …
Although there are pointers on both sides, it seems clear that …
In the end, I have reached the conclusion that …

### Exam help

- ✓ Read the question carefully and choose which two points you want to include. Plan to write four or five clearly different paragraphs.
- ✓ Write ideas for each paragraph, providing reasons to support them.
- ✓ Remember you're evaluating ideas and presenting your point of view. Your conclusion should follow the arguments and evidence you've provided in your essay clearly and logically.
- ✓ Use a formal or semi-formal style. Include a range of vocabulary. Write complex sentences with appropriate linking words and evaluative language.

## Planning your essay

Aim to write four paragraphs.

### Paragraph 1
Introduce the topic in general terms, so the reader knows what the essay will be about. Try to lead in to the discussion in an interesting way without saying what your own opinion is. Raise the main discussion point of the essay, perhaps with a rhetorical question.

### Paragraph 2
Discuss the first note you have chosen. In the sample answer on page 000, the writer has chosen to write about creating trends. Develop your ideas and give examples, if appropriate.

### Paragraph 3
Discuss the second note you have chosen. In the sample answer the writer has chosen to write about increasing awareness. The writer has extended this idea into providing information. Adding to ideas like this is a good way of developing the argument in your essay.

### Paragraph 4
Conclude your essay in such a way that it follows logically from your discussion. The writer has chosen to link the conclusion back to trends, but has extended it to explain why the influence is so strong.

## How to use the written notes

The notes given are short, and you will need to think about ways of explaining and developing them. The opinions you're given may help you with this, but don't use these words or ideas without expanding on them yourself. Here is a possible procedure.

1  Write down the opinions, and think about how they each relate to the question in the task.
2  Add as many of your own ideas to the opinions as you can. For example:

   • **Creates trends:** *people part of a group; pressure to buy certain popular things; expense*

   • **Raises expectations:** *shows ideal and unrealistic lifestyles; makes people unhappy; causes frustration*

   • **Increases awareness:** *gives information; makes people think about things; gives people power to make own decisions*

3  Decide which of the opinions you can say most about. You must be able to organise your ideas into a coherent essay, and your argument should lead to a logical conclusion.
4  Write your essay using the two points you've chosen.

## Checklist

✓ **Content**
Have you given enough detail about the two points you've chosen to write about?

✓ **Communicative achievement**
Is your style and register appropriate for an essay? Are your arguments easy to follow and have you provided evidence to support your opinion? Is your conclusion clear?

✓ **Organisation**
Have you divided your essay into paragraphs, with an introduction and a conclusion?

✓ **Language**
Have you used:
• some complex sentences using linking words?
• a variety of grammatical structures and tenses?
• a range of vocabulary?

## Exam question

You have received an email from an English friend.

Write your **email.**

Write your answer in **220 – 260** words in an appropriate style.

> Hi …
>
> I've got a place on language course at your college for six months, but I need some advice. I'm not sure whether I should take up the offer. Do you think I'll regret anything if I give up six months for this?
>
> The college would fix me up with a flat near the station. Is that a good area? I'm worried about the cost, so I'll need a part-time job. Do lots of students do that?
>
> Let me know what you think!
>
> Carlos

## Sample answer

*This is an email, so use an informal greeting and informal language, including idioms.*

Hi Carlos,

Congratulations on getting on the course! You must be on top of the world! I realise it's a difficult decision to make because six months is a long time to be away from your friends and family, and I understand your fears. Honestly, though, you won't regret coming. When you think about it, employers value people who've experienced life in another country however long or short that experience is. Of course you'd also have good language skills, so in the long-term you'd really

*Give your advice in a friendly way, adding reasons.*

gain from having it on your CV.

*Use clear paragraphs to reflect the different issues you are dealing with.*

You asked about flats near the station. I know in some cities the area round a station can be pretty noisy, but here it's fine. There aren't that many trains and it's very convenient for buses into the town centre. It's close to the college, too, and it's an advantage that there are a couple of supermarkets nearby. I hope you can cook if you're going to live on your own!

Moving on to your next question, it's quite common for students to have a part-time job, which has pros and cons as there aren't many jobs round here. Some find work in the library, and others in the shops, but failing that you can always work in a restaurant. That's what I do, and if you like I can ask about getting you an interview there. Fortunately, it pays quite well, and as a

*Use linking words and a range of tenses to produce complex sentences.*

bonus it would be a useful opportunity for you to meet different people.

So I'd say don't worry and don't think twice – just do it!

Cheers,

## Useful language

**Informal openings**
Dear Carlos,
Hi Carlos,
Hello Carlos,

**Introducing a new point**
You asked about …
To answer your question about …
As to your question about money, …
Moving to your question about …
Finally, you want to know …

**Agreeing to help**
I'm happy to be able to help …
I'll do my best to help you …
I'm not an expert but I can …
If you like, I can …

**Giving advice**
I think it would be good for you to …
I think you should …
Of course you could always …
I'm sure you won't regret it!

**Closing an email**
All the best,
Best wishes,
Regards,
Cheers,

### Exam help

- ✓ Read the instructions and the email carefully, noting all the information you need.
- ✓ Decide what to include in each paragraph. In this case, it's an informal email, but you may be asked to write a formal letter, so think about the style of writing you need to use.
- ✓ Add details of your own to make the email or letter interesting, and try to use a range of complex language.

## Useful language

### Giving background information
The aim of this proposal is …
At the moment …
The current situation is …

### Making suggestions
I propose …
My suggestion is that …
What I propose is …
The best thing would seem to be …

### Explaining potential benefits
It would provide …
One advantage would be …
I would anticipate …
I could be advantageous for …

### Conclusion
In conclusion, I would say that …
To sum up …
On balance …
The evidence suggests that …

## Exam help

- ✓ A proposal is about something that might or should happen in the future. Read the question carefully and plan headings for your proposal. Make sure you include all parts of the task.

- ✓ Consider who you're writing the proposal for, and whether to use bullet points. If you do use them, don't make the language too simple. Use varied complex structures.

- ✓ The purpose of the proposal is to persuade the reader to accept your ideas, so make sure you justify them clearly. Think of interesting details to add, and reasons to support your ideas.

## Exam question

There is a large unused field near your town. There have been plans to use it as a car park, a supermarket or a park. You feel it could be used for the benefit of the town, and decide to write a proposal for the town council. Clarify why you think the field is a wasted opportunity, suggest what should be done and explain how your proposal could benefit the town.

Write your **proposal**.
Write your answer in **220 – 260** words in an appropriate style.

## Sample answer

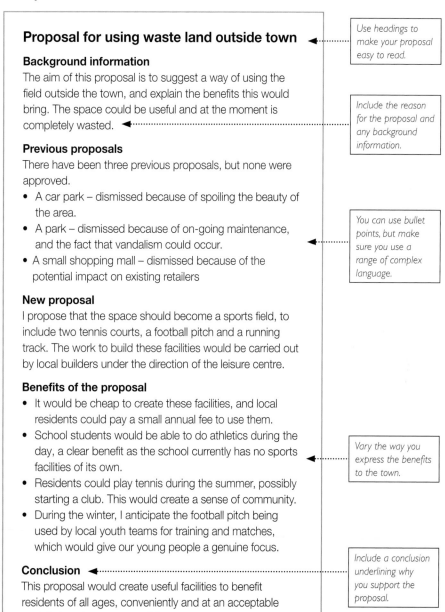

### Proposal for using waste land outside town

**Background information**
The aim of this proposal is to suggest a way of using the field outside the town, and explain the benefits this would bring. The space could be useful and at the moment is completely wasted.

**Previous proposals**
There have been three previous proposals, but none were approved.
- A car park – dismissed because of spoiling the beauty of the area.
- A park – dismissed because of on-going maintenance, and the fact that vandalism could occur.
- A small shopping mall – dismissed because of the potential impact on existing retailers

**New proposal**
I propose that the space should become a sports field, to include two tennis courts, a football pitch and a running track. The work to build these facilities would be carried out by local builders under the direction of the leisure centre.

**Benefits of the proposal**
- It would be cheap to create these facilities, and local residents could pay a small annual fee to use them.
- School students would be able to do athletics during the day, a clear benefit as the school currently has no sports facilities of its own.
- Residents could play tennis during the summer, possibly starting a club. This would create a sense of community.
- During the winter, I anticipate the football pitch being used by local youth teams for training and matches, which would give our young people a genuine focus.

**Conclusion**
This proposal would create useful facilities to benefit residents of all ages, conveniently and at an acceptable cost. I strongly recommend it.

Use headings to make your proposal easy to read.

Include the reason for the proposal and any background information.

You can use bullet points, but make sure you use a range of complex language.

Vary the way you express the benefits to the town.

Include a conclusion underlining why you support the proposal.

WRITING BANK

## Exam question

You have just completed a month doing work experience at a local company as part of your college course. Your principal has asked you to write a report about it. In your report you should evaluate the overall experience, explain which aspect of the work you found most useful, and suggest any changes that might improve the experience for other students on the course.

Write your **report**.
Write your answer in **220 – 260** words in an appropriate style.

## Sample answer

*State the purpose of your report. A report is usually about something that has happened or has been done.*

*Using headings allows you to organise the sections of your report clearly. Give background information to give context to your recommendations.*

*Use complex sentences wherever possible.*

*Give reasons for your recommendations.*

*Include a final section summarising your conclusions.*

### Report on work experience

The purpose of this report is to evaluate my recent period of work experience, identify its use and suggest improvements for future students.

### Background information

As part of my studies in law, I worked at a local firm for a month. During this time, I shadowed a lawyer and worked in the general office.

### Evaluation of the experience

The only work I had done before this was casual employment in a local supermarket. I spent time working in the reception and the general office, and it was beneficial to see at first hand how busy the workplace can be. I shadowed a solicitor, and this highlighted the importance of attention to detail, which I had not fully appreciated before.

Unfortunately, the staff were too busy to spend time with me, so apart from the week when I was shadowing I was left to work things out for myself. They didn't know much about my course and were unable to assign me duties that were relevant. I did a lot of filing, and answering the telephone.

### Recommendations for other students

- There should be greater contact between the college tutor and the company before the period of work experience, so the work given to students could be suitable.
- It would be useful if students could spend a day at the company before starting work, to establish exactly what was expected of them.
- Shadowing is a very valuable experience, and should be part of any future arrangement.

### Conclusion

In spite of my reservations, I found it a very worthwhile part of my course.

### Useful language

**Introducing the report**
In this report I will …
The aim of this report is to …
I have been asked to write a report about …

**Making recommendations**
We particularly liked …
We were most impressed by …
There should be …
It would be useful to have …

**Finishing the report**
Considering everything, I would say that …
To conclude, it would be best if …
Taking everything into account, I conclude that …
The main conclusion of my report is that …

### Exam help

- ✓ Read the question carefully and plan your report before you start to write. Think of the format you're going to use and whether you will use headings. Decide how many headings or paragraphs you will need and calculate where the main focus of your report will be.
- ✓ You should show a range of language, so write full and complex sentences. Use formal or semi-formal language.
- ✓ Include a conclusion, even if it's only a short one.

# Part 2 Review

## Useful language

### Introducing the plot
This tells the story of …
We learn about the relationships …
The book is pure escapism …

### Expressing opinions
I love the way we find out about …
The way character is revealed is …
The story is compelling …

### Recommending
I wholeheartedly recommend this …
If you want to…, look no further …
Would I recommend this? Yes, for …
If you dislike … this is not for you.
You won't believe how good this is.

## Exam help

✓ Read the question carefully and plan your review before you start to write. Think about who the review is for, and what style you're going to use. In this case, it's a website, so the style should be semi-formal.

✓ Plan how to organise the content into paragraphs. You need to inform the reader about the book, give your personal opinion, and say whether you would recommend it and why.

✓ You should try to entertain the reader as well as inform them, so use varied language.

## Exam question

You bought a book after reading reviews of it on a website and it made a lasting impression on you. You decide to write your own review of the book for the website. In your review you should briefly explain what the book was about, consider why it made such a lasting impression on you, and clarify whether you would recommend it to everyone.

Write your **review**.
Write your answer in **220 – 260** words in an appropriate style.

## Sample answer

I chose this book at random when I was in an airport. The cover appealed to me, which may seem to be a shallow reason for choosing a book! Little did I know that reading it would be an engrossing and memorable experience.

*A review should interest the reader, as well as inform them. Try to engage them from the beginning.*

I had never heard of the author, but I was quickly drawn in to the story. It concerns a couple going through a particularly difficult time both emotionally and financially, and is written from the alternating perspective of the husband and wife. This means that the reader is kept in touch with how each of them sees the things that happen, which you might think would spoil the surprises, but no, the writer still manages to shock! This is what made such an impression on me - the idea that I could imagine I understood a person, but could then be shocked by them.

There are some scenes in particular, like when Sue confronts her husband with his dishonesty, that I found myself reading again and again. The language was so vivid and immediate that I felt I was in the same room.

*Give specific examples from the book to support your views, and use interesting language. Don't give away too much detail about the plot so that you spoil it for readers*

Would I recommend the book?  Yes, for anyone who enjoys trying to analyse and understand complex personal relationships. If action-packed blockbusters are your scene, then this is not for you. It's not a fast-moving thriller, and in fact very little actual happens, but as the study of the breakdown of a relationship it is compelling.

*Make your recommendation clearly, and don't be afraid to express your personal views.*

I shall look out for other books by this writer in future.

**Pearson Education Limited**

KAO Two
KAO Park
Harlow
Essex CM17 9NA
England
and Associated Companies throughout the world.

www.pearsonELT.com/

First published 2018
ISBN: 978-1-292-19518-6
Set in Helvetica Neue LT 10/11.5pt and Gill Sans 8.5/10pt
Printed in Slovakia by Neografia

The publisher would like to thank the following for their kind permission to reproduce their texts:

Extract 1.3 from https://www.ft.com/content/4b7634d8-5230-11e4-a549-00144feab7de, © The Financial Times Limited. All Rights Reserved; Extract 1.5 from https://www.ft.com/content/fcd16ff4-e74d-11e6-967b-c88452263daf, © The Financial Times Limited. All Rights Reserved; Extract 1.7 from https://www.ft.com/content/c2dcb73c-9aa3-11e6-8f9b-70e3cabccfae, © The Financial Times Limited. All Rights Reserved; Extract 1.8 from https://www.ft.com/content/636bd31e-f16f-11e1-a553-00144feabdc0, © The Financial Times Limited. All Rights Reserved; Extract 2.2 from http://www.ftsyndication.com/preview.php?id=20161118000IFT_____FREELNCE_4edcadbe-ab84-11e6-9cb3-bb82079_6670.3, © The Financial Times Limited. All Rights Reserved; Extract 2.3 from http://www.ftsyndication.com/preview.php?id=20161021000IFT_____FREELNCE_100c835c-9487-11e6-a1dc-bdf38d4_6670.3, © The Financial Times Limited. All Rights Reserved; Extract 2.5 from Double Trouble, Financial Times Weekend Magazine, 10/10/2009, 40-41 (Blau, R), © The Financial Times Limited. All Rights Reserved; Extract 2.6 from www.telegraph.co.uk/art/what-to-see, Telegraph Media Group Ltd 2016; Extract 2.7 from https://www.ft.com/content/0dc9b416-8573-11e6-8897-2359a58ac7a5, © The Financial Times Limited. All Rights Reserved; Extract 2.8 from https://www.ft.com/content/b538410e-b60b-11e1-a511-00144feabdc0, © The Financial Times Limited. All Rights Reserved

The publisher would like to thank the following for their kind permission to reproduce their photographs:

(Key: b-bottom; c-centre; l-left; r-right; t-top)

**Pearson Education Ltd:** Joey Chan 49c, Alice McBroom 49b, Jules Selmes 50t; **Shutterstock.com:** 390130 52t, AVAVA 50c, axle71 53b, bikeriderlondon 53t, Inc 52b, oliveromg 49t, 50b, peresanz 53c, Catalin Petolea 52c

All other images © Pearson Education

Every effort has been made to trace the copyright holders and we apologise in advance for any unintentional omissions. We would be pleased to insert the appropriate acknowledgement in any subsequent edition of this publication.